LAUGHING MATTERS

LIVE CREATIVELY WITH LAUGHTER

MARIANA FUNES

Life does not cease to be funny when someone dies, anymore than it ceases to be serious when someone laughs. George Bernard Shaw

Newleaf

Newleaf
an imprint of
Gill & Macmillan Ltd
Hume Avenue
Park West
Dublin 12
with associated companies throughout the world
www.gillmacmillan.ie

© 2000 Mariana Funes
0 7171 2893 8
Designed by Vermillion Design
Print origination by Carole Lynch
Printed by ColourBooks Ltd, Dublin
Index by John Loftus

A catalogue record is available for this book
from the British Library.

5 4 3 2 1

CONTENTS

In Praise of *Levitas*   v

Dedication   vii

Acknowledgments   viii

The Executive Summary or Can I Be Bothered to
Read this Book   ix

Chapter 1
Where Do the Other 385 Go?   1

Chapter 2
I Laughed Till I Cried: The Physiology of Laughter   18

Chapter 3
Playing with our Pain: Permission to Laugh   58

Chapter 4
Ways to the Inner Laughing Place: Choosing our Beliefs   96

Chapater 5
Ha Ha! Leading to Aha: Laughter is Creativity   137

Chapter 6 My Gift of Laughter   185

Appendix 1
Dingbats   211

Appendix 2
Should We Be Working ... or Larking?   213

Appendix 3
The Laughter Workout   223

Appendix 4
Your Living Theory of Laughter   227

Notes   228

Index   237

Contact Information   244

IN PRAISE OF *LEVITAS*

I take my laughter very seriously. Long before I knew about the health-giving effects of laughter I used to make it my aim in my daily interactions with people to share a smile, a chuckle or a laugh with them before moving on to the busy demands of my day. I judge the success of my interactions with others by the extent with which I am able to share laughter with them. I am not talking about jokes or comedy here. This is not about being a comedian. I am talking about what can be called conversational laughter, and the kind of setting where such laughter occurs is one were you can be playful. It may interest you to know at this early stage in our exploration of laughter that less than 20 per cent of our laughter is in response to formal efforts at humour.[1]

Laughter connects us to people beyond the superficial. It did not surprise me to learn that the Greeks pursued *levitas* and not *gravitas* as the source of wisdom, and that they spent time reflecting on and theorising about the role of laughter in a healthy society. Their general conclusion was that it should be regulated because it had a powerful effect on those citizens who chose to indulge in laughter. The role of the court jester was born then and it did not have the pejorative connotations that it has in certain circles today. Court jesters were known to understand the human mind and spirit in such a way that those who came into contact with them had to have purity of intention or risk being damaged by the perceptive nature of their comments.[2]

People who had an in-depth understanding of life, and therefore great wisdom, were said to have the gift of *levitas*. The term means lightness and I do not believe it is chance that achieving the highest degrees of wisdom in the east is labelled 'enlightenment'. Laughter is the response that we have to understanding life devoid of pretence. When we finally 'get it', say the wise in the east, there is only one thing left for us to do: laugh. This may be what is behind the finding that a dying patient's face will sometimes light up in what Zen calls the 'original face' just before death. The use of the word 'light' in English to mean the opposite of 'dark' as well as the opposite of 'heavy' combines in one word the idea of illumination with that of lightness of spirit. In Spanish there are two separate words for these concepts – *liviano* and *iluminado*. I wonder what we could deduce from this particular linguistic difference, as to the nature of the views on laughter within the cultures in which these languages are spoken.

So, to get back to my story, having been told all my life that the only worthy goal in my professional life should be the pursuit of *gravitas*, I now know that what made me successful was my steadfast refusal to let go of my gift of *levitas*.

What follows are the many ways I have discovered that laughing matters in our lives – how to give ourselves permission to laugh in the face of so many social pressures to de-value that which is at the source of our understanding of reality and of our ability to be 'real' in the sense that the Velveteen Rabbit was real.[3] I hope you can laugh and learn with me through the pages of the book.

DEDICATION

To you mum for preserving the essence of what makes me real as you brought me up to be who I am today

To you Marcelo for helping me develop my sense of the ridiculous and for understanding the Joke of Life. I now know that there are only three points I need to remember …

To you Kevin for keeping me real each day I know you, as we share the pain of life in laughter and this creates an ever-stronger bond between us

To everyone who likes to laugh with me. I thank you for guiding me to this little book

To Michael and Michael for making it a reality and to you Peter for working on a Sunday!

Annette, thank you for opening that door

And Fiona, I'm sorry you had to wait so long!

ACKNOWLEDGEMENTS

The author and publishers wish to thank the following for permission to reproduce illustrations:

Adbusters Media Foundation for the spoof ads on pages 208–209; Blue Dolphin Publishing for the cartoon on page 196; 'Living Lightly' Magazine for the cartoon on page 188, drawn by Tom Percival.

Every effort has been made to trace copyright holders of materials used in this book. The publishers will be glad to hear from any copyright holders who were not found before publication.

THE EXECUTIVE SUMMARY OR CAN I BE BOTHERED TO READ THIS BOOK?

The aim of this book is to bring out into the open one of life's best-kept secrets – one that we all know and yet feel strangely embarrassed to talk about. The secret is this: Laughter is good for us. When we laugh we feel better. So what? you may be asking, I knew *that*! Yes you did. You do. But knowing it and doing it are not the same thing. Psychologists sit around counting the numbers of times we laugh, and you know something? As we grow up we learn clear rules that actually stop us from using laughter to help our well being.

This book is about the locus of control for your laughter coming back to you rather than being determined by the external world. It is about you becoming laughter-independent and developing your own guides as to how you use laughter in your life.

Interested in reading on yet? Here is a sneak preview of what the pages of this book contain. I do hope you will be tempted to go on this laughter journey with me.

Chapter 1 Where do the other 385 go? Psychologists tell us that we lose 385 laughs between childhood and adulthood. Where do they go? And more importantly, how can we get them back? We begin our search by exploring what makes us stop our 'human laughter response', as laughter is referred to by serious laughter researchers, at the times when we most need it. Laughter is good for our body and for our mind. It is our beliefs about appropriateness that keep us from using laughter to maintain a balance in our emotional life, which is the link between body and mind – the only way we have of 'getting into' the body-mind conversation.

The 385 laughs have been lost because we have forgotten this language of the connectedness between body and mind and have bought into an educational system that only values serious pursuits, where serious is defined as the opposite of playful. We stop playing and start the serious business of life. This book argues that adults have forgotten about matters of consequence, as the Little Prince reminded us, in their pursuit of seriousness, and have confused seriousness with thoroughness.

And we are mistaken. Laughing matters because it provides us with a tool to close the gap between doing and knowing and thus bring more of who we are to our interactions.

Chapter 2 I Laughed Till I Cried: The Physiology of Laughter In this chapter we explore the physiological bases for laughter. You may wonder why this is important. I am convinced that the most effective attitude-changer is the 'look-at-what-laughter-can-do-for-your-body' speech. Here are some of the key points contained in this chapter:

☺ Your tears contain more immunoglobulin after laughter. This antibody is the first line of defence against certain viral and bacterial infections.

☺ When you laugh your mouth also contains more immunoglobulin.

☺ You brain and body produce beta-endorphins – powerful endogenous opiates which help relaxation and pain reduction.

☺ Enhanced immune function has been clearly demonstrated in laughter.

☺ Stress hormones are reduced. Cortisol levels increase in an unhealthy way during stress. They decrease significantly with laughter.

☺ Blood pressure increases during laughter and drops below resting level afterwards.

☺ There is reduced muscular tension after laughter.

☺ Air is expelled from your lungs at really fast rates when you have a good chuckle. Your body gets thoroughly oxygenated. This is good for thinking clearly and for aerobic fitness.

☺ Laughter has an anti-inflammatory effect. It can reduce inflammation and help relieve pain in arthritic conditions.

So much for the body. We also ask 'when do we laugh?' and explore many laughter theories. We learn about emotional literacy. We need to develop a language to explore life below our necks. We are a body and not just a brain. Laughter helps us make the body-mind connection.

Laughter helps us detach and not take life so personally. As this ability develops within us, we lose the need to construct a completely cohesive narrative of our behaviour from day to day. We learn that we are full of paradox and inconsistency and that this is okay. It is not something to hide from others or from ourselves. This is the junction of our being where development and growth can happen, the junction where integration of mind and body can be achieved on a daily basis, thus leading us to better health.

Chapter 3 Playing with our Pain: Permission to Laugh You may think it odd for me to suggest that it is possible for us to play with our pain. When we are in the depth of pain, be it physical or emotional, we rarely see that we can choose to direct our attention in ways other than towards our suffering. And yet we can. Seriousness does not stop because we laugh and funniness does not stop because we cry. They co-exist in our life and we need to give ourselves permission to access both when we need to.

We do not get to choose if we want pain in our lives. The only thing that we get to choose is whether we access that inner laughing place to help us keep our emotional life in balance, despite the pain. In this chapter we learn about the role of true play in regaining that balance.

William Fry defines humour as play. 'First, humour is play. Cues are given that this, which is about to unfold, is not real. There is a "play frame" created around the episode.' From this we could argue that there is no hurtful humour. If we put a 'play frame' around it, any topic can be used to help us laugh. To some extent this is true. But there is one crucial point missing from this interpretation. We must have permission to put a play frame around a topic, in order to avoid hurtful laughter.

As we learn to re-connect with our laughter and to play with our pain with permission and compassion, we need to know more about how we process our emotions. Some ways of dealing with our emotions are healthy and others are not. We look at our emotional process as going through two interconnected cycles. One I call the reality cycle, because it leads us to having free attention to sense the world in the present moment. The other I call the magical thinking cycle, because it leads us further and further away from sensing the present moment.

In this chapter I share with you some communication strategies that will help you develop your laughter quotient. We explore the idea of a living theory of laughter, through some clear examples, and give you guidelines to develop your own. If you are to be laughter independent you will need to have a developed sense of what laughter means to you in your life.

Chapter 4 Ways to the Inner Laughing Place: Choosing our Beliefs
Here we explore the nature of our beliefs and how they can help or hinder us from achieving the results we want in our lives. We discuss the laughter barriers – games we play that get in the way of us finding laughter in our lives:

☺ Why are you laughing? It's not that funny.

☺ That's enough; let's get back to work!

☺ I love him because he makes me laugh.

☺ How can you laugh at a moment like this?

☺ They laughed a lot, but I don't know if they learned.

☺ I can't help it. It's just the way I am.

We explore ways that may help us do an 'inside job' on our model of the world, to allow us to respond to outside circumstances in more sustainable ways. We learn about the language of laughter, ways to learn to choose the meaning that experience has for us.

Chapter 5 Ha ha! Leading to Aha: Laughter is Creativity We can be creative in our lives when we have the gift of perspective, but more importantly when we are able to generate many different ways of perceiving the world in a purposeful way. Laughter leads to new insights and gives us access to our creative self. This chapter will give you practical ways to enhance your relationship with your creative self. It will help you understand why it is important to have the courage to 'play the fool' if you are to keep your soul alive through your life, and have the quality of life you deserve.

Creativity is the process of using our imagination to continue the world, creating in the process of further elaborating on the world itself. Creativity is a process of acting in the world to continually put together the familiar in unfamiliar ways and of finding existing pattern rather than imposing pattern. Creativity is a matter of survival and its development is no laughing matter. I will help you make some connections that will allow you to use laughter to develop your ability to live the creative life. Creativity is a gift we all possess but don't all use, and so is laughter. The similarities don't end there.

We are curious animals and can only survive in our world if we have ways of satisfying our curiosity. True play is the way in which human animals do this. Our society does not value true play for adults. We are taught to strive, to pursue serious goals. We therefore become impatient, take shortcuts and are then surprised when our performance drops.

If we develop our ability to find laughter in our life we can get closer to our creativity because laughter is our link with true play. True play is our link to the kind of thinking that allows us to view life as a constant process of redefinition. Laughter can be a sign that we are learning new patterns, that we have grasped a new way of seeing something. In short, laughter can be a measure of how much and how actively we are participating in the process of the creation of every day. So, we design our course on thinking creatively, 'Creativity, the art of everyday making'. We sign up for a few imaginary modules that will help us lead creative lives. I give you some specific examples of how to do this in your life should you have the inclination. Firstly, I introduce you to surrealist games and end the chapter with some practical examples of creative people. People who are able to use the whole of their life as a pool for making non-habitual associations. People who view their work as an opportunity to create every day.

Chapter 6 My Gift of Laughter You will find in the final pages of the book a collage of ideas and thoughts and ramblings which help me connect with my own inner laughing place. We go from the ridiculous to the sublime, and back again. It's all contained within the same soup of experience and it is okay for you to choose what to focus on at any given time. Serious frames and play frames are valid filters for life. What matters is whether it is you or other people who determine the way you look at your own life. If it is you, you have genuine choice. If it is others, you may find your-self at the end of your life with somebody else's life flashing in front of you!

There is also a laughter workout in Appendix 3, inspired by the Laughing Clubs of India. We always start the second day of my 'Laughing Matters' workshop with it. Its aim is to learn to laugh for no reason at all. We laugh for 30 minutes unconditionally. We laugh as Dr Kataria, the creator of the laughing clubs, suggests, 'because we can, not because of some outside stimulant. We want to liberate laughter from conditions.' It is a delightful way to start the day.

IS THIS BOOK FOR YOU?

Yes, if you want to have more laughter in your life; if you intuitively know that 'laughter is good for me', but want to know why. This book is for those who want the answer to the perennial question, 'Why are you laughing?' The book will provide practical experiments and strategies to help you regain the courage to do what works: Laugh more, even when society may be saying that laughter is not an 'appropriate' response. This book is for you if you want to understand who determines 'appropriateness' and want to have the courage to determine what 'appropriate' means for yourself.

WHY WILL IT HELP YOU?

The book will help you because it will get you to re-think and re-assess your attitude to a most fundamental human response: Laughter. As people become more able to generate laughter in their own lives and allow themselves to laugh when they choose, they close the gap between the person they are on the 'inside' and the person others think they are. This increases people's ability to be more fully themselves in more situations in their lives. What this will achieve for you over time is an increased ability to deal with the stresses of life.

HOW IS IT GOING TO HELP YOU?

This book will help you by providing simple and clear ways to change some of your long-established patterns and to become more aware of how these patterns contribute to your life being the way it is. The aim of the book is to provide a challenge to the received view on laughter as an unimportant part of human experience. This will allow you to make new choices, if appropriate, on how you can live your life out loud – expressing the uniqueness that is you.

There are many models and many arguments about how Laughing Matters in our lives. I offer you in the following pages the sense I have made of what I have learned so far in the hope that it encourages you to bring out into the open your own laughter theory. I know you have one.

CHAPTER 1

WHERE DO THE OTHER 385 GO?

It is said in psychological folklore that children laugh 400 times each day whereas adults only laugh 15 times. The search is on for those 385 laughs that have disappeared between childhood and adulthood. My interest lies, not in why we turn away from laughs, but in how we can rediscover a few, to help us live lighter lives.

Knowing that laughter makes us feel better, and actually using laughter, are not always the same thing. When asked, I say that laughter is good for me and that it makes me feel better. But when I reflect on how many times I laughed this week, I realise I hardly laughed at all. I obviously decided that laughter would have been inappropriate in the serious situations I have been involved in during the week. I did not laugh because the situation did not warrant it. I have rationalised opportunities for laughter as serious situations and on reflection discover that I have not laughed in years. And that is how the 385 laughs are lost.

It is an unfortunate quality of the human cognitive apparatus that we can hold contradictory living theories. We act in one way, but believe that we do not. This is because as we grow older we realise that we can create our own rules for living. We no longer have to use the categories others give us and we make up our own. We decide what category a given action belongs to. We thus develop the ability to generalise our actions, to 'say one thing and do another' and, when others point out possible inconsistencies, insist, 'That did not count!'

Psychology has gone a long way towards finding explanations of how we organise our internal world. I would like to take a detour at this point to tell you something about these explanations. I will then come back to connect this with the action of laughter and the beliefs we have about laughter. I will argue that we absorb certain beliefs about laughter and act on them unconsciously to stop ourselves from laughing, and that these beliefs can co-exist with our belief that laughter is good for us and that it makes us feel better. This is how knowing and doing are not the same thing. They must, however, become the same if we are to gain control of our laughter to enhance our well being. So let's start the detour with an explanation of the ways in which we decide on the meaning of signs.

ARBITRARY MEANINGS

The study of signs is called semiotics, and any sign is fair game for study. What does a sign mean? A No-entry sign, a number, a letter, words, symbols, anything that stands for something other than itself is the subject of semiotics. So, as I write this the day before mother's day, I may choose to take mum a bunch of flowers to symbolise my love for her. The flowers are not my love. They represent it. We have agreed meanings in our society about these kinds of symbols. Signs often represent what is intangible, something like love.

Language is a set of signs which point to different experiences but *are not* that experience. So the words which point to a given experience will depend, for example, on which language I was born into. A man called De Saussure spoke of this phenomenon as 'the arbitrariness of the sign'. Why is this important? Laughter is a sign, a sign that has meanings assigned to it. We don't really know how symbols gain their meaning. If it were just a matter of pointing to clear links between the sign and what it stands for, we probably would not need a whole science dedicated to the study of the sign. Language is not tied to the world in a straight-forward way. The world is not as solid as we once thought it was and language is linked to it much more loosely than we once thought.

Laughter as a sign can have many different meanings conferred on it. The mappings are not very clear; neither are they few or conscious. Hence it is sometimes difficult to make decisions about when it is appropriate to use this particular sign. In a sense this book is an attempt at making some of these implicit links explicit, to allow us to make decisions about the right context for our laughter.

Try this activity before you continue reading. Make a list of what makes you laugh. Get hold of your diary for the past four weeks and use it as a memory jog to help you compile a list of specific events that got you laughing.

Your list will include a huge variety of events, if you are still finding laughter in your life. Sometimes what we discover is that the list does not even include the prescribed 15 laughs we are 'supposed' to have. We will come to explore what you can do about this and why you should bother doing anything about it. For now suffice it to say that a potential list could look something like this:

☺ Being tickled by someone you love

☺ Seeing a magician at your child's party

☺ Playing a game and winning

☺ Hearing a joke

☺ Listening to someone ruin a joke

☺ Observing someone who does not get the joke

☺ Meeting an old friend

☺ Anticipating some pleasant activity in the future

☺ Feeling embarrassed

☺ Meeting the gaze of a friend and laughing for no reason at all

☺ Covering up your anger at something that someone has said

☺ Smoking marihuana

☺ Feeling nervous or anxious.

I could go on for pages and pages and the only pattern appears to be that there is no pattern. We seem to use the reflex of laughter

in so many situations that it is difficult to work out any correspondence (and certainly no one-to-one correspondence) between the
sign and what the sign stands for. The exploration of laughter in
this book will, hopefully, go some way towards providing a map
for these correspondences.

PATTERN RECOGNITION AND G-MODE

The process of assigning meaning to signs is not as transparent as
we would wish. For example, we don't really have a clue why we
choose to attach the combination of the letters B L U E to the
colour blue. It is not surprising that we sometimes are unaware of
the reasons for choosing one sign over and above another. Choosing
to shake someone's hand rather than kiss him or her once on the
cheek, for example, is not a choice in any real sense of the word.
We often find ourselves in a confused frame of mind when the
choice we have made happens to be different from that of the
person we are greeting. The choice is partly culturally based, partly
based on our educational background, our gender and our perception of the formality of the situation. We do at least recognise
that both signs are a means of greeting another person.

What is this process whereby we act on certain information we
receive from our environment without any understanding, on a
conscious level, of why we have acted in a particular way? As
humans, we are never happy to be reminded that there are aspects
of our humanity that do not conform to our vision of ourselves as
rational animals. We like to believe that our behaviour is determined by a chain of cause-and-effect, building up into a sequence
which becomes an interesting narrative when we explain our
actions to friends over dinner. Indeed the legal concept of the
'reasonable' man is based on this particular illusion. There is a great
deal of data accumulating in cognitive science and psychoneuroimmunology[1] that has demonstrated beyond any 'reasonable
doubt' that our actions are determined by much more than the
rational narrative which we avail of to explain them.

The argument is put in its strongest form by a neuroscientist called Michael Gazzaniga who argues for what is known as selection theory and against our ability to alter certain evolutionary patterns which we utilise in order to survive. He even suggests that learning is no more than discovering the patterns which are 'pre-existing in our brains'. The data he uses to support his theory is truly convincing and its implications far-reaching. 'Learning may be nothing more than the time needed for an organism to sort out its built-in systems in order to accomplish these (survival) goals.' We learn to survive, and possibly 'all that we are doing in life is catching up with what our brain already knows'. Educators therefore can do no more than put learners in environments which stimulate their pre-existing patterns. In other words, we develop by recognising pattern and those patterns are not always in our consciousness. We can, and do, act on patterns without knowing it. Much of our behaviour is structured (in the sense of following a pattern) but unconscious (in the sense of not having a presence in our conscious mind). So the term 'unconscious understanding' is quite relevant.

Laughter is an example of human behaviour that is clearly observable, but not in terms of the patterns that lead to it. We often try to imprison laughter in our limited models of how we think. We may find ourselves asking, 'Why are you laughing?' Of course the inevitable result of such a question is for the other person to stop. The question is an example of our assumption that everything that happens happens for a reason. Our model of thinking cannot assimilate the notion of that which is other-than-rational. If we are going to be able to actively use laughter to enhance our well being we need to know that thinking and learning are more than an explicit set of rules which we follow in an orderly manner.

One of the jigsaw pieces that we need for our exploration of laughter and why it matters, is a review of what counts as thinking.[2] In order to become laughter independent we must expand our understanding of how we think. So, let's review our living model of humans as thinking machines. We have two modes of thinking. We favour one as thinking and dismiss the other as intuition. D-mode thinking (where the D stands for deliberate) and G-mode (where the G stands for gap) are the two modes. Let's look at their qualities side by side:

D-mode Thinking	G-mode Thinking
☺ Cognitive conscious	☺ Cognitive unconscious
☺ Explicit and articulate	☺ Unconscious intelligence
☺ Language and symbols	☺ Takes time: Dare to wait
☺ Goal is certainty	☺ Goal is to 'mess around' with the problem
☺ As I think so it is	☺ Perceive beyond initial evaluation
☺ Consciousness is essential to action	☺ Acts without consciousness
☺ Purposeful	☺ Playful
☺ Operates at the speed of language	☺ Develops know-how
☺ Slower but methodical	☺ Non-verbal: Fast and can deal with complex pattern
☺ Procedural	☺ Stable over time
☺ Finds solution	☺ Handles complex pattern identification and acts on those patterns!
☺ Habit	☺ Originality
☺ About evaluation of ideas	☺ About generation of ideas

There are clear distinctions between these two thinking modes. They are a fundamental part of our ability to make sense of the world and we need to develop both to be all we can be. The issue here is that each mode of thinking is good for different purposes.

D-mode will work for me when I'm dealing with the kind of problem that can be broken down into parts, that has a known solution and that requires me to follow specific steps to arrive at it. G-mode, on the other hand, works well for me when I need to develop practical mastery and innovation. G-mode absorbs unconscious pattern, while D-mode creates a narrative about those patterns that arrive into consciousness.

> *It's not as if intuition [G-mode] happens in one place, and logical thought [D-mode] happens somewhere else. It's that intuition and logical thought are different modes of functioning of the brain as a whole.* Guy Claxton

Both modes have upsides and downsides. The key is to select the mode that is appropriate to what my environment is demanding of me. For example, D-mode can become detached from experience because it is good for transcending particular contexts through abstraction. G-mode may not transfer a given skill to a new context because it has absorbed so much detail of the pattern within a particular context.

We could say that D-mode addresses the actions that are geared towards meeting our basic drives of fear and hunger; we need to be able to know what to do in a new situation and we must use what we have learned from other situations to help us survive. But Arthur Koestler talks about a third basic drive in humans: the exploratory drive, which in everyday language we might simply call curiosity. G-mode helps us fulfil our exploratory drive; it is our curiosity that keeps us making connections and developing new patterns that our D-mode can then use. G-mode teaches us about the source of our experience; D-mode helps us develop conscious awareness of our unconscious understanding. We need to value both equally and develop both equally, if we are to have access to all of our thinking abilities to live the lives we want to live.

Our culture encourages us to spend many years honing our D-mode skills and de-valuing G-mode. We have been misled into believing that science is all D-mode and that science is giving us the results we want. Yes, D-mode has a role to play in science when explanation is the focus. Almost all accounts of scientific achievements have, however, relied on G-mode to get to the formulation of a question.

> *You suddenly see: 'It must be like this.' That's intuition . . . if you can't convince anybody else. This certainly happened to me in the work for which I got the Nobel Prize. It took me years to get my stuff across.* Sir Neville Scott

So the upshot of all this is that you need both modes and that you are not thinking effectively unless you use both. The problem is that our educational system teaches only one mode and that as a society we are becoming more and more driven to get quick results at work and in the rest of our lives. We assume that D-mode will get us there quickly. Yes, and it needs G-mode as the foundation for knowing what is the 'stuff to get across' to others. If we focus on the places in our lives where there is laughter, we will discover that the keyword 'playful' is also connected to those very same aspects of our lives. Playfulness is the link between laughter and effective thinking. We have lost the 385 laughs because we have lost play and have over-emphasised D-mode.

Laughter belongs to the right hand column and not the left. Laughter helps us access that right hand column for many different purposes and this happens through what I have been calling unconscious understanding. This is why we sometimes cannot verbalise our reasons for laughing. We know so much more than we know we know.

Laughter is our signal that we have made a new connection. We suddenly perceive something in a new way. This is the essence of G-mode thinking. We will come back to this in later chapters. For now, let me emphasise that there is a strong connection between laughter and freedom of thought and expression. It is because of this connection, and because we need shared rules to function as a society, that we control laughter through implicit rules of appropriateness.

Laughter as a sign has many different meanings. Some are made explicit and some are acted upon without conscious awareness. Laughter focuses our attention on G-mode, that aspect of thinking that we often dismiss as not serious or purposeful enough to achieve the tight deadlines we are working towards. The paradox of the centipede becomes all too real when we try to apply D-mode to the kind of life experience that requires G-mode. The centipede stops being able to walk when asked to work out which leg is the first to move. Laughter is a very serious matter. It will connect us with the type of thinking that we need to manage in today's complex world. As a society, we have reached the limit of analytical excellence and need to expand our notion of what thinking is.

Laughter can be a way of developing G-mode and it is this mode of thinking that needs our attention if we are to discover more of the pre-existing patterns that will help us survive and thrive in our environment. Our ability to discover new patterns is not just relevant to scientists: it is the essence of what makes us human.

SOME MORE THOUGHTS ON HOW LAUGHTER HELPS THOUGHT

There is much more I could say about how we think, but I want to focus my effort on just a few key points that cognitive science has determined with reference to thought. I will then move on to argue that all of the qualities that research identifies as necessary to effective learning are also the qualities that help you get in touch with more laughter in your life. We will explore this in depth later in relation to living creatively with laughter, but here I want to summarise some research findings and interesting experiments.[3]

☺ Neurological studies show that it is the conscious aspects of memory, perception and action that are lost first in brain-damaged patients. G-mode stays with us through injury and there is some evidence to suggest that injury dis-inhibits laughter.

☺ The ability to do a job develops much faster than the ability to articulate what we are doing. In the same way, we can laugh and not know why.

☺ We can make use of pattern and not know it consciously. Laughter is a reflex action, often triggered without conscious understanding.

☺ We can detect, learn and use patterns *and* deny their existence when presented with evidence of use; as in the old story of the daughter who said to the mother, 'Why is it that you always clear out the garage when it is time to do your tax returns?' – a pattern which, of course, the mother denied vigorously.

☺ Our *confidence* in our abilities follows explicit knowledge rather than know-how. We need D-mode to have confidence in what we know. Laughter helps us bring together both modes of thought and, therefore, increases our confidence in our abilities.

☺ There is a delay between perception and conscious awareness – a delay of 350 milliseconds, in fact. Movement starts before we are aware of it and laughter is a kind of movement. The initiation of movement is G-mode and this may be the reason why at times we are unable to answer the question, 'Why are you laughing?'

☺ Competence is negatively related to people's ability to articulate rules of behaviour. We can laugh and think without articulation, and this is an integral part of our cognitive abilities.

☺ Conscious beliefs are not changed by acting on contradictory patterns learned in G-mode: Espoused and embodied theories can co-exist in contradiction. We can believe that laughter is good and not find any laughter in our daily lives. This too is an integral part of our cognition.

☺ D-mode can get in the way of a whole variety of mental functions because it devalues affect and sensory data that may contain useful patterns. Affect (a fancy word for emotions) is a gateway to G-mode thinking. We talk of hunches and intuition as based in our affective realm. Laughter is a gateway to our affective realm and helps us develop emotional literacy.

Laughter is, in short, a way into more effective thinking once we understand that the notion of thought has to be updated to include G-mode.

And here are some principles for effective learning, which you will note lead to creating an environment where play (doing an activity for its inherent value) is supported and hence where laughter can naturally occur:

☺ We must educate people about the different ways of knowing: D-mode and G-mode are fundamental to learning.

☺ Interacting with the world without 'figuring it out' can deliver understanding and performance beyond what is possible in D-mode.

☺ Thinking is not just conscious reflection. There is cognitive value in confusion and not-knowing.

☺ Safety is key to fostering the development of G-mode.

☺ Certain kinds of cognitive processes take time!

☺ Develop resilience. In order for learning to occur people should be allowed to grapple with confusion without withdrawing. Frames of play are useful here.

☺ Beliefs unconsciously drive behaviour. A deterministic view of mind (saying to oneself 'I can't change this') will work against developing resilience (saying to oneself 'I'll keep trying until I fail better').

☺ We should cultivate all ways of knowing and not seek to replace one with the other.

☺ Imagination and visualisation lead to effective learning.

☺ A 'could-be' approach leads to flexibility and creativity, to continuously asking the question, 'How could I do this?' Or as somebody famous once put it, 'I did not know I could not do it.'

☺ Learning must be grounded on experience that is relevant to you. We can learn pattern and use it without awareness.

☺ Involve D-mode and E-mode equally.

☺ Affect is a way to embed learning.

☺ Always attend to your mental state before starting to learn any specific content.

☺ Pay attention to the power of suggestion. Use language that assumes learning is easy and enjoyable.

☺ Involve the whole of the mind/body system in the learning experience.

☺ Laughter increases your sensory awareness.

☺ Use a variety of mediums to explore the kernel ideas of the content you want to learn.

The argument that we act on unconscious pattern, and that G-mode is fundamental to our ability to learn and to think,[4] focuses our journey into laughter. As we explore laughter and find ways to allow it into our lives more often, we now know that we are learning about a new language of thought; a language that helps us create a more holistic view of people as thinking beings; a language that integrates rational thought with unconscious understanding and with emotional literacy. Laughter is a sign that, if practised, can mean all of this and much more.

WHO CONTROLS WHEN WE LAUGH?

I want to highlight a number of points about laughter:

☺ We have very definite and implicit rules about laughter.

☺ These rules are internalised and acted upon without conscious awareness.

☺ These rules are external to the individual.

☺ The locus of control as to when laughter can be used is with the larger group; peer pressure will often determine appropriateness.

☺ There are many conflicting rules about the use of laughter.

Society frowns at the idea of laughter being used indiscriminately. We have a set of norms for its appropriate use. We create the illusion that there is a right way to use laughter and a wrong way. The wrong way is relative to my culture and to the setting I find myself in, not in any way absolute. If I have no awareness of the patterns I'm acting on, that make it 'wrong' to laugh at a funeral but 'right' to laugh at a comedy store. I'm using laughter according to somebody else's rules and these rules, on conscious examination, may or may not fit for me.

The attempt to control laughter is not new. Plato in his *Republic* warned us against it. He said that it weakened character and confused the mind. Comedians are often the targeted groups in totalitarian states and are forced to use humour only in the service of the goal of the state. It is said that Hitler was also aware of the capacity of laughter to hurt the Third Reich and that he held 'Joke Courts'. The purpose of these was, for example, to punish those that had the audacity to name their dogs Adolf![5]

The implicit assumptions that are made to control our laughter are some version of the following: 'But laughter is weakness, corruption, the foolishness of our flesh'.[6] Rather than run the risk of being perceived in this kind of light we choose not to laugh in many situations. I will argue later that a lack of awareness that we are responding to these societal messages will negatively affect our mental and physical health.

The process of indoctrination or brainwashing, where a person is forced to pursue a particular view and becomes unable to deviate from it, is said to be doomed to failure if the subject laughs. William Sargent states that if the subjects laugh at any point in the process, 'the whole process is wrecked and must be begun all over again'.[7]

Governments that use these procedures in the hope of controlling their citizens in the service of totalitarian aims, would do well to listen to the advice of Michael Gazzaniga:

> It is my hope that you will discover, as I have, that all the ways that human societies try to change minds and to change how we humans truly interact with our environment are doomed to fail. Indeed, societies fail when they preach at their populations. They tend to succeed when they allow each individual to discover what millions of years of evolution have already bestowed upon mind and body.

And one gift that has been bestowed on us is that of laughter.

LAUGHING MATTERS AND IT IS YOURS TO USE!

The breadth of people who have written on the subject of laughter is inspiring: Aristotle, Plato, Hobbes, Freud, Kant, Schopenhauer, Spenser, and Koestler. The latter dedicated the first 90 pages of *The Act of Creation* to the Jester and his role in creativity. We have a huge number of researchers in many fields exploring the role that laughter plays in the well being of our body and mind. Koestler talks about it as a 'luxury reflex' that can only have evolved in humans at the stage of 'cortical emancipation' where we became able to perceive our 'own emotions as redundant, and make the smiling admission "I have been fooled"'. He further states that laughter could only arise 'in a biologically secure species with redundant emotions and intellectual autonomy'.[8]

In my time working with laughter 'formally', running workshops, writing and speaking to the press, I have found that laughter serves many purposes for us humans. One key purpose is that it keeps us free from the tyranny of our past and of our society. 'For as long as the tyrant cannot control the minds of free men, they remain free.'[9] Bob Newhart comments on how laughter abounded behind the Iron Curtain and in POW camps. Victor Frankl explores this theme in depth when describing life in a concentration camp. We will come to this later in the book.

Laughter is a way of dealing with that which we cannot explain. Laughter gives us distance. It allows us to step back from an event over which we have no control, deal with it and then move on with our lives. In later chapters we will look at how all of this supports our ability to be creative in our lives. You will learn about bissociative thinking as the basis of the creative process.

Laughter can also define our sanity. Our ability to bissociate independent universes of discourse functions only when we are mentally healthy. Koestler defines this ability as the key to laughter and creativity. The moment clinically depressed patients laugh is a moment of breakthrough towards healing. Until that point they have perceived their world as a constantly frightening, unfriendly place. When a schizophrenic is asked, 'What would you do if you had wings?' he typically answers, 'But I don't have wings.' He can only look at life literally and is unable to use the 'act-as-if' frame that is the hallmark of human imagination.[10] We will use this frame when we discuss the notion of learning to play with our pain and discovering ways of bringing our beliefs up-to-date with who we are today.

A great book by Erasmus titled *In Praise of Folly* states the following: 'No society, no union in life could be either pleasant or lasting without me' — *me* of course being folly. People who can laugh tend to be less self-indulgent and more pragmatic in their world-view. They can be more humble when successful and less defeated in difficult times. Certainly there are more important things in life than finding laughter in what we do, but I cannot imagine anything else that makes my life more worth living. One of the most persuasive things that gets in the way of us living the lives we want to live, is that we are too serious. We confuse seriousness with thoroughness in what we do. It is this confusion that leads us to lose touch with that 'inner laughing place' that can give our lives its joy.

> *Laughter frees us from vanity, on the one hand, and from pessimism on the other by keeping us larger than what we do, and greater than what can happen to us. A. Penjon*[11]

This book is about the locus of control for your laughter coming back to you rather than being determined by the external world. It is about you becoming laughter independent and developing your own guides as to how you use laughter in your life. We act without awareness and our G-mode way of thinking is not as well developed as it needs to be. We can hold a belief that says that 'laughter is good for us' and yet act in the world as if the other 385 had been irretrievably lost. We know one thing in D-mode and do another through G-mode. Learning to act differently takes time. We need to discover pattern, but our busy lives allow less and less time to just 'mess around' with a theme and thus allow patterns to emerge. I hope that as you take the time to mess around with this exploration of laughter, you will learn new patterns.

In what follows you will learn about the world that is hidden under that harmless little sign of laughter. The human laughter response, as psychologists like to call it, is noticeable, tangible and very much measurable. Let's go on an exploration of what laughter means and what we can do to find the laughs from our childhood that we have lost.

Knowing and doing are not always the same thing. Laughing matters because it provides us with a tool to get closer to doing what we know and thus bring more of who we are to our interactions with other people.

CHAPTER 2

I LAUGHTED TILL I CRIED:
THE PHYSIOLOGY OF LAUGHTER

The first step in our exploration is to understand the physiological bases for laughter. You may wonder why this is important. My experience has convinced me that the most effective attitude-changer is the 'look-at-what-laughter-can-do-for-your-body' speech.

In this chapter, let's look at you laughing from two different perspectives: your body in laughter and the effects of having laughed for say, ten minutes.

For the lazy ones amongst us, who can just accept that there is good evidence to support certain claims, I highlight below what happens to your body when you laugh:

☺ Tears in your eyes contain more immunoglobulin — an antibody which is your first line of defence against some viral and bacterial infections.

☺ Your mouth also contains more immunoglobulin. This indicates enhanced immune function.

☺ Your brain and body produce beta-endorphins, internal opiates which help you to relax and reduce pain.

☺ Stress hormones produced by your adrenal glands are reduced. Cortisol levels increase in an unhealthy way during stress; they decrease significantly with laughter.

☺ Blood pressure increases during laughter and drops below resting level afterwards.

☺ There is reduced muscle tension after laughter.

☺ Air is expelled at very fast rates from your lungs and body when you have a good chuckle. Your body gets thoroughly oxygenated. This is good for thinking clearly and for aerobic fitness.

☺ Laughter has an anti-inflammatory effect on your joints and bones; it can reduce inflammation and help relieve pain in arthritic conditions.

In summary, your physical and mental being benefits each time you find laughter in your day.

YOUR BODY IN LAUGHTER

We must first address some matters of definition. When we talk about laughter, what exactly do we mean? When I talk about laughter mattering to our well being, I refer to any response to an external or mental stimulus that involves the muscles of the face in what is known in the literature as the 'enjoyment smile' configuration.[1] As well as the basic response, the intensity of the response has to be considered. At one end of the continuum there is the subtle smile, Gioconda style. We need a way of talking about what else is on that continuum. We can take a continuum from certain laughter studies[2] and define differences in intensity as follows:

☺ Grade 1: no response

☺ Grade 2: smiles of different magnitudes

☺ Grade 3: laughs ranging from normal to moderate

☺ Grade 4: the explosive laugh.

So the term laughter in this book will be used to refer to any grade of response intensity, except grade 1. We will be exploring laughter in general and not just laughter in response to a particular stimulus such as humour. In the literature laughter and humour are often used interchangeably. Even if, as Apte suggests in his book on the cultural aspects of humour, laughter is the external mani-festation of humour, we laugh in response to much more than humour and often laugh in response to nothing at all. Laughter is itself sufficient to generate laughter. The contagious nature of laughter is obvious to us all but if you need convincing, there is 'serious' research that demonstrates this fact.[3]

We laugh when embarrassed, when uncertain, when sad, when we just want to 'go along' with what has been said. Laughter has emotional, cognitive and environmental antecedents and con- sequences and I do not intend to narrow my definitions in this book but to explore the collage of all that a laughter experience involves from as many perspectives as I can. So, laughter includes smiling and is a human response that is present in many human situations not all of which are to do with humour. Most laughter is spontaneous and not in response to jokes.

Let's look at the pattern of occurrence of laughter to give you an idea of just how difficult it is for those of us who want to take laughter seriously. Laughter can be elicited as a reflex, as in tickling. It can be a voluntary reaction to an event, as in hearing a joke. It can be the result of pathology, as in brain damage. It can be the result of the unexpected. The list could go on and, to quote Donald Black, it is this 'chameleon nature that defies scientific interpre- tation'.[4] Black also says, 'Laughter as a behaviour has many causes, including humour, incongruity, relief, a sense of well being,' and theories that involve all these elements have been developed to explain the experience of laughter. We will review some of these in the sections that follow.

Let's look in more detail at your body in laughter. We start with the face through the words of Pollio et al,

> As the upper lip is raised in smiling, it partially uncovers
> the teeth and also brings about a downward curving of
> the furrows which extend from the wings of both nostrils
> to the corners of the mouth. This, in turn, produces a
> puffing, or rounding out of the cheeks, on the outer side
> of the furrows. Creases also occur momentarily under the

eyes, and in older people it is possible to see 'laugh creases' at the side edges of the eye sockets. The eyes themselves undergo a general change which can be best described as becoming bright and sparkling.[5]

Such a long description for something that takes so little time when we do it! And that is only what goes on in the face. Now a challenge to you.

Try this activity: Describe your body in laughter. Take a blank piece of paper and continue the description above to include all that you notice in your body when you laugh.

Some of the qualities you will have included may have been:

☺ Tears in your eyes and eyes swelling up slightly. The tear glands work to keep your eyes moist and increased circulation produces vascular changes.

☺ Muscle contractions in different parts of your body, but mainly around the torso due to the altered breathing. Lungs have been clocked expelling air at over 60 miles per hour.

☺ General loss of muscle control. This can cause you to 'fall off your chair' laughing.

☺ A significant change in breathing.

You may also have found out that it was impossible to do the task of describing your body in laughter and laugh at the same time. This is the conundrum of all laughter researchers. There is an immense amount of research on laughter, and none of it will make you laugh! Just like the quote above, it all seems a rather laborious process to go through to explain the unexplainable. To some extent this describes the activity I am engaged in as I write this book. Please bear with me if some of its content seems to be breaking up the essence of the activity of laughter: spontaneity. Another aspect of this essence is paradox. Laughter is found at the junction of two apparently incompatible universes of discourse.

Scientific explanation and a good laugh seem to me an example of this incompatibility. Let's now move on to a different aspect of your body in laughter, the sound of laughter.

THE SOUND OF LAUGHTER

We talked about the air being expelled from the lungs at speed. The sound is produced by inhaling air, which is then followed by:

> short, interrupted, spasmodic contractions of the chest and especially the diaphragm, hence, side splitting laughter. The 'belly laugh' is caused by large abdominal body circumference changes brought about by the inspiratory-expiratory cycle. The primary component of laughter is an abrupt, strong expiration at the beginning, followed by a series of expiration-inspiration microcycles with interval pauses. This is superimposed on the larger respiratory pattern so that the rhythmic sequence and frequency of expiratory-inspiratory excursions determine an individual laughing style.[6]

The sound of your laughter, then, will be determined by all those cycles and micro-cycles working together. Complicated, ugh? Well, we can complicate it even more. William Fry has explored seven parameters that will further determine 'the respiratory components of mirthful laughter' and these are: duration, magnitude, predominance of different components, frequency, sequence, rythmicity and excursion levels. The interaction of all these parameters is what generates the almost infinite variation of laughs.[7] This analysis gets highly technical and comprehensive. However, the important point to note is that there are many different parameters that will determine the characteristic sound of your laugh and that researchers are working towards creating a vocabulary to describe these differences. It is a bit like creating a grammar of laughter.

We can all speak grammatically, yet few of us can be explicit about the rules of grammar. We can all laugh, yet few of us know the grammar of laughter though some of us want to create one. An interesting example of this kind of work is provided by Robert Provine who takes an anthropological approach to the study of laughter. He analyses laughter with a sound spectrograph that translates a sound into an image showing the frequency and intensity of sound over a period of time. His paper reveals the image that contains 'the distinct signature of laughter'.[8]

> A laugh is characterised by a series of short vowel-like notes (syllables), each about 75 milliseconds long, that are repeated at regular intervals about 210 milliseconds apart. A specific vowel sound does not define laughter, but similar vowel sounds are typically used for the notes of a given laugh. For example, laughs have the structure of 'ha-ha-ha' or 'ho-ho-ho,' but not 'ha-ho-ha-ho.' There are intrinsic constraints against producing such laughs. Try to simulate a 'ha-ho-ha-ho' laugh – it should feel quite unnatural. When there are variations in the notes, they most often involve the first or last note in a sequence. Thus, 'cha-ha-ha' or 'ha-ha-ho' laughs are possible variants.[9]

Explosive laughter, our grade 4, has a strong harmonic structure. Each harmonic is a multiple of a low core frequency. Females have a higher core frequency (about 502 hertz) than males (about 276 hertz). A deep belly laugh or a high-pitched titter: according to Provine all laughter is a variation of this basic form. We recognise laughter as such because of this basic structure and know it to be 'as different as possible from screams or cries of distress'.[10]

And here are some more interesting observations that Provine shares with us on the sound of laughter:

> The notes and internote intervals carry most of the information that allows us to identify a sound as laughter. If the sounds between laugh notes are edited out of a

*tape recording – leaving the notes separated by intervals
of silence – a laugh still sounds normal. The internote
time interval carries information, but the internote
expiratory sounds do not. If the notes are removed from
a recording and the gaps between intervals are closed,
all that remains of laughter is a long, breathy sigh. The
stereotypic structure of a laugh is, at least in part, a result
of the limitations of our vocal apparatus. It is difficult
to laugh with abnormally long note durations, such as
'haaa-haaa-haaa,' or abnormally short durations (much
less than 75 milliseconds in length). Likewise, normal
note durations with abnormally long or short internote
intervals do not occur. Try to produce a natural laugh with
a long internote interval, such as 'ha————ha————ha.'*

*As with the natural rhythms of walking or running, there are
only so many ways to laugh. The structural simplicity of a
laugh is also suggested by its reversibility. A short segment of
laughter – 'ha-ha-ha' – played backward on a tape recorder
still sounds rather like 'ha-ha-ha.' Indeed the sound spectrum
of a laugh is similar whether scanned from left to right or
from right to left – a laugh note has a high degree of temporal
symmetry. Yet one aspect of a laugh that is not symmetrical
is its loudness. Laughter is characterised by a decrescendo in
which the laugh notes that are late in a sequence are usually
lower in amplitude than earlier notes (presumably because
we run out of air). Recordings of laughter played backward
produce a bizarre-sounding crescendo.*

Provine's work takes the study of laughter into the 1990s and he
has the gift of making it understandable and testable in our
everyday experience.

Try this activity before you read on. Experiment with the different
parameters of laughter described in the quote above. Get to know
the distinctive style of your own laughter. Can you write a para-
graph in answer to the question: What is my laughter style?

So next time you see a child having a good belly laugh, you can reflect on just how complex the response is, even if all you try to do is describe what you see going on in the child's body from the outside.

We will now move on to look at laughter from a different perspective: the effects of laughter. We will look at what happens to our body after we have laughed. Our focus now will become more internal rather than observable behaviour. If you thought that grading systems for the human laughter response and sound images for the structure of laughter were weird and wonderful ways to study this phenomenon then what follows will be way off your weird-and-wonderful scale. Just be thankful that you were not a subject for any of these studies!

THE EFFECTS OF LAUGHTER

When researchers study the effects of laughter it is generally laughter in response to watching some funny film that is measured according to a complex formula. They test various physical measures before and after watching the funny material and using control groups for comparison; i.e. people who are not watching the funny material. There are many variations on the experimental method: laughing researchers, confederates who are planted in the experimental situation by the researchers, injections of hormones to create arousal, alarms that go off on unsuspecting subjects at different times of the day to get them to record mood changes and laughter frequencies . . . I told you it gets weirder.

The lengths we will go to for the sake of seeking explanation never ceases to amaze me and I have been in the business of explaining human behaviour all my life. You will find below a summary of the key effects of laughter that these strange experimental methods have found and I will tell you about some of the more interesting experiments to help your after-dinner conversation if nothing else! Each subtitle tells you in essence what the effect is, so you don't have to read the whole section unless you are interested in that particular effect.

LAUGHTER RELIEVES PAIN

Annette Goodheart uses laughter for pain relief with people who have had surgery. She suggests that as you focus your laughter on the area that hurts, you can achieve significant pain relief. Norman Cousins first called the attention of the medical community to the therapeutic effects of laughter in 1979 when he described how he used laughter during his treatment for ankylosing spondylitis, a serious arthritic condition. He put himself on a systematic programme of laughter by watching films which he found funny. He says:

> I made the joyous discovery that 10 minutes of genuine belly laughter had an anaesthetic effect and would give me at least two hours of pain-free sleep. When the painkilling effect of the laughter wore off, we would switch the motion-picture projector again, and, not infrequently, it would lead to another pain-free sleep interval.[11]

Cousins used bone sedimentation rates to measure the antiinflammatory effect which laughter had and found that these decreased significantly over time, even though his prognosis had been poor. He was able to return to work and lead a reasonably normal life until his death. He awakened the interest of the medical community in the potential therapeutic use of laughter in arthritic conditions. I have seen Annette Goodheart work with arthritic joints and provide significant pain relief to those she works with. The extent to which the effect she is able to elicit is a placebo cannot be determined by observation. If laughter gives the patient access to a means of pain relief, then we may not need to ask much more about what parameters are at play – If what we are after is pain reduction and not explanation; and if the effect can repeatedly be accessed by the patient.

Suzanne Herchenhorn[12] has studied the relationship between focused laughter therapy and rheumatoid arthritis. She found that frequency, intensity and duration of laughter affected the intensity of pain and pain bothersomeness. Laughter reduced pain intensity, but had more of an effect on how much the pain bothered the patient. Her results show that, at the very least, we feel the same amount of pain and simply care less about it when we laugh! I know that I, for one, would rather feel the pain and not care – at least there is one less thing to worry about.

A different, and less tongue-in-cheek, interpretation of Herchenhorn's results, which is more in line with other physiological findings, is that the laughter produces what is known as endorphins to generate the pain reduction. Endorphins are the body's own painkillers, our own version of what doctors use to treat extreme pain – morphine and its derivatives. Endorphins are very special chemicals, produced by the body to ease the pain of injury and help us withstand physical stress. They also make us feel euphoric, which may account for the feeling of not caring about the pain. Our awareness of endorphins is relatively new. We have only been aware of them for the past 20 years or so. Researchers came across these special chemicals when studying the brain's reaction to opiates (opium, morphine, and heroin). Opiates reduce pain but have also been linked to suppressed breathing and heart rate. They can also, depending on the amount given to a patient, kill.

These endogenous opiates, the endorphins, so called because they are formed within the body, have dedicated cells that behave as receiving stations. The cells are called neuro-receptors and also process exogenous opiates. Endorphins have potent analgesic properties and have been found in all animals. They have a different effect on us humans, however. They not only block pain but they also mediate emotions.

The limbic system is the message centre for our emotions. It takes information from the senses and transmits it to the rest of the body. It contains 40 times as many opiate receptors as other parts of the brain, and there are also other key areas of the body where high concentrations of opiate receptors are found. These areas relate to the integration of sensory data and also to our intuitive perception of many emotions. So as endorphins turn our pain off, they also turn our emotions on.

Laughter can be thought of as the electricity that kick-starts the switch. However, it is not the only method for activating endorphin production. Many methods, some of which are centuries old, are believed to achieve this goal, e.g. acupuncture, relaxation, meditation, exercise, and hypnosis. All of these methods have been linked to an increased ability to laugh and we will return to some of them later in the book. The common link, at a purely physiological level, may be the production of endorphins.

As stated earlier, your breathing changes significantly when you laugh. Candace Pert makes the link between rate and depth of breathing and changes in the quantity and the kind of peptides, of which endorphins are an example, produced by the body. She tells us that there is 'a wealth of data' that shows this connection. Through conscious control of our breathing, she says, we can cause peptides to 'diffuse rapidly throughout the cerebrospinal fluid' as we attempt to re-establish balance. The yogi and the woman in labour use this as a technique, she reminds us. Laughter may be another way of regulating our peptide flow.

New research has also suggested that endorphins interact with the immune system. An excessive amount of morphine reduces the body's ability to cope with infections and can reduce the activity of disease-fighting white cells. This may suggest to us that it is important to find the right balance in endorphin production. Laughter is good, but too much laughter may not be. This finding may support the notion that we should enhance naturally-occurring laughter in our lives, rather than create artificial situations to generate it. We will come back to the immune system connections below.

So, at best laughter can reduce pain through helping us produce endorphins. The endorphins are produced naturally when we experience pain, but laughter can give its production a boost. At the very least, laughter can help us reduce pain bothersomeness. This pain relief therapy costs us nothing, is not addictive and can have many positive effects on those around us.

If you are the kind of person who finds it difficult to make a laughter connection with a painful situation, this book will help you forge that link. You may also be interested in reading the wealth of material that is available on the therapeutic use of laughter in serious illness and terminal disease. If someone dying of cancer can find that inner laughing place to help his or her quality of life, then how arrogant of the rest of us to think that our situation could not lend itself to laughter! As Alfred North Whitehead said, 'Nothing, no experience good or bad, no belief, no cause, is in itself momentous enough to monopolise the whole of life to the exclusion of laughter,' or in the words of a patient:

> Of course serious illness is serious! Why else would they call it 'serious'? That is all the more reason to avail yourself of every advantage — Including laughter.[13]

I want to finish this section on pain with some titles of books that look at the use of laughter to support the seriously ill or dying:[14]

☺ *Intoxicated by my illness*

☺ *Love, laughter and a high disregard for statistics*

☺ *Telling tombstones*

☺ *Nothing is not funny*

☺ *Healthy irreverence: Humour in stories of illness*

☺ *Not now . . . I'm having a no hair day*

☺ *How am I going to find a man if I'm dead?*

☺ *Surviving the cure: A time to laugh*

☺ *The last laugh*

☺ *Laugh your way to health*

☺ *Laughing through tears: Laughter as a resource in grief*

☺ *Laughter in hell: The use of laughter during the holocaust*

☺ *God said 'ha'*

☺ *Sometimes we laughed*

☺ *I've got cancer, but it doesn't have me*

☺ *Laughs in the face of Aids*

I could go on. The value of laughter to us when we are in pain has been demonstrated in more ways than I can mention in this book. My focus is on how we can find 'that inner laughing place' more often in our daily lives. If you still need convincing of the importance of this ability you would do well to remember that sometimes, during critically painful times, the only thing left for us to do is laugh! This list helps me remember to stay humble when I convince myself that my many 'serious' activities are so serious that there is no room for laughter. If there is laughter in death and dying, I can surely find laughter in other life matters of much less finality.

LAUGHTER REDUCES STRESS AND ENHANCES IMMUNE SYSTEM ACTIVITY

In this chapter we are focusing on the physical aspects of laughter. That laughter helps us deal with stress mentally is something that most of us do not need to be convinced about. The problem is that at the most stressful times we do not contact that laughing place within us and judge that time to be inappropriate for laughter. Well, next time you find yourself making that particular judgement bear in mind what I'm about to tell you about the connection between laughter and stress.

Stress creates unhealthy physiological changes. The link between stress and high blood pressure, muscle tension, a suppressed immune system, and many other changes has been clearly demon-strated over the many years of research on this topic. Well, we also appear to have proof that laughter has just the opposite effect on our body.

Lee Berk, who works at Loma Linda University School of Medicine in the Department of Clinical Immunology, has shown that the experience of laughter lowers cortisol levels, increases the amount of activated T lymphocytes, increases the number and activity of natural killer (NK) cells . . . And so it goes on. In short, laughter stimulates the immune system, off-setting the immunosuppressive effects of stress. The studies he has carried out demonstrate that there are clear physiological benefits in using laughter to handle stress. Let's look at these effects in more detail:

☺ During stress, the adrenal gland releases corticosteroids that are converted to cortisol in the blood stream. High levels of cortisol have an immunosuppressive effect. His research has shown that laughter lowers cortisol levels thereby protecting our immune system.

☺ NK cells attack viral or cancerous cells. They are key in the prevention of cancer and laughter increases their activity. Cells in our bodies are constantly changing and produce potential carcinogenic cells. A healthy immune system mobilises these NK cells to destroy abnormal cells.[15]

☺ T cells are activated in laughter, which provide lymphocytes that are ready to deal with potential foreign substances. Berk studied interferon-gamma (IFN), an immunoregulator, produced by activated T cells and natural killer cells. IFN is active in fighting viruses and regulating cellular growth and serves to ensure co-operation between certain cells in the adaptive immune response.[16]

To get an idea of the kind of painstaking research that Berk and his colleagues have carried out read this extract from one of their research papers, where they elaborate on the relationship between IFN and laughter:

Our study's experimental group consisted of ten healthy, fasting male adult volunteers. They viewed a preselected 60-minute mirthful/humor video. Blood samples for gamma interferon were obtained through an IV catheter. We measured IFN before the subjects viewed the humor video (baseline), during (intervention), after (recovery) and also the following day. With exquisite attention to detail, we utilized state-of-the-art methods to quantify measurements and sophisticated statistical multivariate analysis of variance (MANOVA) to interpret the results. Baseline data were gathered 10 minutes prior to viewing the video; intervention measures were taken 30 minutes into the video; and recovery measures were collected 30 minutes after the video ended. The following day (twelve hours after viewing the video) samples were again taken.

Examining baseline data and contrasting it with intervention measurements (while viewing the humor video) demonstrated significant increases in IFN (p<0.001). Comparisons with 'recovery' (p<0.001) and 'next day' samples (<0.001) also revealed significant increases. Within the group, effects over time by repeated measures (MANOVA) showed a significant increase for IFN (p=0.02) in experimental subjects. Plasma volume, hematocrit and total serum protein showed no significant change over the time points studied.

Therefore, these data suggest that the eustress paradigm of the mirthful laughter metaphor may be capable of modifying components of the immune response by increasing production of IFN and subsequent immunomodulation.

Lee Berk and his colleagues at Loma Linda are not alone in having found connections between our emotional state and stress tolerance. Here is a summary of some other research findings:[17]

☺ Steven Locke at Harvard University has shown that NK cell
activity decreases during periods of heightened life changes
that are accompanied by severe emotional distress. People
going through life changes, but who experience less
emotional distress have normal NK cell activity.

☺ Michael Irwin showed that NK cell activity decreases during
depressive responses to life changes, allowing us to
hypothesise that it is our approach to these life changes
that seems the more significant parameter. Laughter can
allow us to refocus our attention to generate responses to
life changes that are other than depressive.

☺ At Ohio State University School of Medicine, Janice and
Ronald Glaser have studied cellular immunity response
patterns in medical students before exams. They showed
a reduction in helper T cells and lowered NK cell activity
during the high anxiety moments just before an exam.

Another set of relevant research findings has to do with salivary
immunoglobulin A (IGA) which is our first-line of defence against
infectious organisms that get into our bodies through the respiratory tract:

☺ In 1987, at the State University of New York, it was found
that salivary IGA levels were lower on days of negative mood
and higher on days with positive mood. A positive mood can
be measured by amount of laughter activity, and the laughter
may be achieving one of two effects: a demonstration of a
joyful state or the release of other emotions that are unrelated
to joy. We will look at theories of laughter below and explore
the notion of positive and negative emotions in greater detail.
The point is that the effect found may be about emotional
flow and not about the quality of the mood.

☺ Other researchers at Western New England College found
that people showed an increased concentration of salivary
IGA after viewing a funny video. Again the laughter response

was a significant parameter. We can conclude that laughter enhances IGA activity.

☺ Herb Lefcourt, from the University of Waterloo, found that subjects who tested strong for appreciation and utilisation of humour had a higher enhancement of salivary IGA after viewing a humorous video than subjects who tested weak. We can assume from these findings that they laughed more and hence the levels of IGA were even higher.

The past 10 years of research have helped us to understand the strong connections that exist between the body and the mind. The summary of research I have given you up to this point gives you a flavour of the kind of connections I am talking about.

The new science of psychoneuroimmunology is focusing even more on the exploration of these connections. Our emotions affect our immune system and there are those that say that endorphins and other neuropeptides are the physiological substrates of our emotions. We will explore the significance of this below when we look at the work of Candace Pert, the researcher responsible for the discovery of the opiate receptors. We talked about her earlier when we discussed the pain-relieving effect of laughter. She argues that what we perceive as mind is the movement of different neuropeptides informing our bodies about what physical changes to bring about based on our emotional state.

Receptor sites are important as an information link between the brain and the immune system. Emotions trigger the release of neuropeptides from neurones in the brain. These chemicals then enter the blood stream and bind to receptor sites on the surface of immune cells. When this happens, the cell's metabolic activity can be altered in ways that are conducive to health or ill health.

Unlike the position taken by Norman Cousins and other researchers, Pert's theory suggests that emotional health is determined by free flowing neuropeptides and not by the replacement of one type of emotion (e.g. negative emotions) by another (e.g. positive emotions). Her research is part of the psychoneuroimmunology field, and it explores the communication links and relationships between our emotional experience and our immune response as mediated by the neurological system.

If the emotions we experience directly affect our immune system and laughter allows us to perceive and appreciate the incongruities of life as well as providing a release valve for pent-up emotions, then laughter can create neurochemical changes that buffer our immune system from the detrimental effects of stress. These changes take place not because we are happy and then laugh but because laughter has a re-balancing function in our body irrespective of our perceived reason for laughter. As the old saying goes: 'We don't laugh because we are happy; we are happy because we laugh.'

> *Mirthful laughter serves to modulate specific immune system components somewhat like the conductor of an orchestra. The conductor has the option to increase tempo and volume, rendering the music more harsh, rapid and less harmonious. Incorporating the metaphor of mirthful laughter, however, the conductor can calm the tempo, enhance sonic integration, and ensure a melodious performance.* Lee Berk

Hans Selye defined stress as the rate of wear and tear in our body as it adapts to change or threat. Finding laughter in a situation is a powerful antidote to stress. Conscious access to that laughing place within gives us the ability to release our attention from distress and find the delight and joy that exists in our experience side-by-side with our pain. This is a great way to take care of ourselves during stressful times.

In sum, laughter provides a cathartic release, a purifying of emotions and a release of emotional tension. Laughing, crying, raging, and trembling are all cathartic activities which can unlock energy flow.[18] These cathartic activities have more to do with re-balancing our bodies than with an expression of happiness. It is this re-balancing that appears to counter the effects of stress, whether the laughter is an expression of joy or anger or fear.

LAUGHTER HELPS US DETACH FROM PROBLEMS

Laughter can give us power over our circumstances. Laughter can give us a different perspective on our problems and as we detach, we feel protected and in control. Victor Frankl talks about how he could tell early on who would survive the experience of the concentration camp, by monitoring their ability to find laughter in their terrible circumstances. He talks about the skill of finding laughter in all of life as that skill which is developed while mastering the art of living and, he says, the art of living can be practised even in a concentration camp.

> I never would have made it if I could not have laughed; it lifted me momentarily out of this horrible situation, just enough to make it liveable.

Bill Cosby, in very different personal circumstances, has put the same idea in a succinct way: 'If you can laugh at it, you can survive it.' If the locus of control is internal, then a person will feel a greater sense of power and be much more likely to avoid burnout or survive critical life experiences. Let's look at some of the background to this generalisation.

It was Selye who said that the interpretation of stress is dependent not only on an external event, but also on individuals' perception of the event and the meaning they give to it. The way you perceive a given situation will determine whether you respond to it as threatening or challenging. As different people respond differently to the same environmental stimuli, some people seem to cope with stress better than others. Suzanne Kobassa has defined three 'hardiness factors' that can increase a person's tolerance to stress and prevent burnout: commitment, control, and challenge – all three modelled in a profound way by Victor Frankl in his life experience. Let us look at them in a more mundane context.

If you have a strong commitment to yourself and your work, if you believe that you are in control of the choices in your life, and if you see change as challenging rather than threatening, then you are more likely to deal with stress effectively. A key theme in the literature is that a causal factor in burnout is a sense of powerlessness. This is how we come full-circle to the notion that laughter, as it detaches you from your problems, helps you manage those very problems in a healthier way.

You cannot always control what life sends your way, but you have a much more significant degree of control on how you handle it than you may think. An image that has always helped me in difficult times is that of sailing: I have no control over the winds, but I certainly can adjust those sails! The use of laughter represents cognitive control. We cannot control events in our external world but we have the ability to control how we view these events and the emotional response we choose to have to them. Laughter involves the whole brain and helps to balance activity in both hemispheres. Sven Svebak[19] has shown that there is a unique pattern of brain wave activity during laughter and other researchers have shown that in response to jokes, brain activity seems to unify as the joke requires the involvement of both the emotional and cognitive parts of the brain.[20]

WHAT HAS LAUGHTER GOT TO DO WITH CRYING? EMOTIONAL LITERACY

I hope that at this stage you are determined to go looking for a few of those 385 laughs. I now want to widen our discussion to exploring the reasons why we laugh. This is going to take us on a tour through many different answers to this question, before pulling them together to enable you to hone your emotional literacy. I then want to suggest some practical ways for you to attend to life below your neck, which is where G-mode resides. One interesting fact to remember as we go on our emotional tour is that the site of laughter and crying in the brain is in the same tiny spot in the hypothalamus. Stimulate the site at one frequency and you get tears; stimulate the same site at another and you get laughter.[21] This finding will be of interest as we explore the cathartic and non-specific effects of laughter on our emotions.

So, why do we laugh? We all know that some things do make us laugh. It is harder to say what it is that these things have in common. Theories of laughter are many, and are attempts to answer this question. We can divide the theories into three simple categories: superiority theories, incongruity theories, and relief theories. We will explore all three generally and focus on one particular relief theory to help our exploration of emotional literacy.

WE LAUGH WHEN WE FEEL SUPERIOR

Very often we laugh at people because they have some failing or defect, or because they find themselves at a disadvantage in some way or have suffered some small misfortune. The miser, the glutton, the drunkard are all stock figures of comedy; so is the henpecked husband or the man who gets hit with a custard pie. We laugh, too, at mistakes: at schoolboy howlers, faulty pronunciation, and bad grammar. These are all fairly crude examples, but it may be that even more subtle laughter is a development of this, and that the pleasure we take in laughter derives from our feeling of superiority over those we laugh at. According to this view, all laughter is caused by the kind of derogatory humour of these examples.

Thomas Hobbes (1588–1679) is the originator of this theory:

> Laughter is a kind of sudden glory.

He adds that we laugh at the misfortunes or infirmities of others, at our own past follies, provided that we are conscious of having now got over them, and also at our unexpected successes. Superiority theories seem to leave out of account one very important element in humour: incongruity. It is the sudden mixing of contrasting attitudes that causes laughter.

For Alexander Bain all laughter involves the degradation of something. He says that we need not be directly conscious of our own superiority and that it need not be a person that is derided: it may be an idea, a political institution, or anything that makes a claim to dignity or respect. According to all superiority theories, laughter originates always from looking down on a thing or a person, and so it is judged inferior by some standard.

Henri Bergson gives a clear instance of a superiority theory. Bergson's core value is adaptability. So what is laughable is 'something mechanical encrusted upon the living'. The typical comic character is a man with an obsession, e.g. Don Quixote. He is not flexible enough to adapt himself to the complex and changing demands of reality. As a typical example of comic rigidity, Bergson cites the story of the customs officers who went bravely to the rescue of the crew of a wrecked ship. The first thing they said when they got the sailors ashore was: 'Have you anything to declare?' Here we have the automatic persistence of a habit of mind, regardless of altered circumstances. We laugh at rigidity and feel superior when adaptability is perceived as good and we feel ourselves to have it. Laughter is society's defence against the eccentric who chooses not to adjust himself to its requirements.

This has some resonance with the ideas we will be exploring in chapter 5 about how play can help us develop our adaptability and creativity.

WE LAUGH WHEN WE PERCEIVE AN INCONGRUITY

Many writers on humour and laughter have refused to accept the view that at the centre of laughter there is always a degradation of some kind. They hold that incongruity is quite distinct from degradation and that incongruity, not degradation, is a central feature of all laughter.

Incongruity is often identified with the notion of 'frustrated expectation', a concept we owe to Immanuel Kant, who says that laughter arises 'from the sudden transformation of a strained expectation into nothing'. More is implied here than surprise. Kant suggests that laughter emerges from the violent dissolution of an emotional attitude. This is done by the abrupt intrusion into the attitude of something that is felt not to belong there, of something that comes from another part of our mind. Anger rather than joy seems to be the emotional subtext for laughter here.

Based on this view, what is essential to laughter is the mingling of two ideas which are experienced as dissimilar. More laughter happens when whatever originates it brings to light a true connection between two things regarded with different attitudes, or when the connection forces on us a reversal of our values. The theory of creativity that we explore in chapter 5, that of Arthur Koestler, is also an incongruity theory of laughter. If we look at Oscar Wilde's witticism, 'Work is the curse of the drinking classes' we find it funny, not just because of its close resemblance to the wording of the conventional remark which it replaces, 'Drinking is the curse of the working classes,' but because it gives us a quite different, but equally appropriate, evaluation of the social fact it refers to.

Herbert Spencer thinks that all laughter can be explained as a response to descending incongruity. Spencer, like Bain, believes that incongruity involves a contrast between something dignified and something trivial or disreputable, but for Spencer it is the incongruity, and not the degradation, that is the important feature. Spencer wants an answer to a question overlooked by others. Why should the perception of incongruity lead to the bodily manifestation of laughter? His answer is that laughter is an overflow of nervous energy, and that the abrupt transition from a solemn thought to a disreputable one leaves us with a fund of nervous energy which needs to be expended in laughter.

Laughter, according to incongruity theories, emerges from finding the inappropriate within the appropriate. It is not merely that unexpected connections are found between apparently dissimilar things: our notions of propriety are also involved. In any community certain attitudes are felt to be appropriate to some things but not to others; and there develop stereotypes of such figures as the typical politician, or poet, or maiden aunt, and so on. A comedian can bring to light certain inconvenient facts which shatter attitudes and puncture stereotypes.

WE LAUGH WHEN WE NEED EMOTIONAL RELEASE

Since laughter emerges, often, from that which calls conventional social requirements into question, it may be regarded as giving us relief from the restraint of conforming to those requirements. The relief may be only temporary. A risqué joke, for example, is not usually a serious challenge to conventional morality, but it does enable us to air the sexual impulses which society makes us repress. Moreover, people who have been under stress will sometimes burst into laughter if the cause of the stress is suddenly removed. It may be, then, that a central element in laughter is neither a feeling of superiority nor the awareness of incongruity, but the feeling of relief that comes from the removal of restraint. Putting a frame of play around social restraints can allow us to speak the unspeakable and this can lead to a feeling of relief.

This theory has been reinforced and brought into prominence by Sigmund Freud.[22] Freud himself regards laughter as a means of outwitting the super-ego, his name for the internal inhibitions that prevent us from giving in to many of our natural impulses. It is not only our sexual impulses that are repressed by the super-ego, but also our malicious ones. In this way Freud is able to account, not only for indecent jokes and for the appeal of comic characters like Falstaff who ignore conventional moral restraints, but also for the malicious element in humour to which superiority theories call attention.

According to Freud, the super-ego will allow us to indulge in these forbidden thoughts only if it is first beguiled or disarmed in some way. The beguiling is done, he thinks, by means of the techniques of humour: such devices as punning, representation by the opposite, and so on. An insult, for example, is funny if it appears at first sight to be a compliment.

To take another example, the witticism from Wilde must be regarded, from this viewpoint, as allowing us to give vent to suppressed wishes about work and drink or to suppressed malice against the working classes. The super-ego is first taken by surprise because we appear to be merely repeating a conventional remark, and is then diverted by the discovery that a very slight rewording of this remark enables us to express quite different sentiments. If we use the more up-to-date model of the cognitive unconscious to explain Freud's position, we say that D-mode is cheated into accepting something that emerges from the cognitive unconscious, our G-mode way of thinking. As we notice that we have allowed the unthinkable into our consciousness, we laugh.

The intellectual pleasure of playing with words and ideas and of finding unexpected connections, regarded by the incongruity theories as an essential element in laughter, finds a place in Freud's theory as a means of tricking the super-ego. Freud explains this by adopting Spencer's physiological explanation of laughter. Laughter results from the economising of nervous energy and from giving vent to our repressed desires. It is interesting to note, in relation to this last point, that damage to the higher centres of the brain dis-inhibits the laughter response that is associated with the pathological laughter often present in brain-damaged patients.[23] It is just possible that D-mode thinking, located in the higher brain centres, censors G-mode thinking in order to manage our cognitive load.

Laughter and crying are adaptive processes: A model for catharsis

Annette Goodheart has adapted the Freud/Spencer model of emotional release. She provides us with an updated model for our emotional life. Catharsis, she argues, can re-balance our bodies and our minds. As we experience the pressures of life, on a daily basis, this pressure causes tension and pain. The pain can be physical or mental. It is stored up in our bodies and needs release. Our bodies have been provided with the means to release the stored-up pain, through tears, laughter, yawning, shaking and temper tantrums. All of these processes are labelled cathartic processes, ways of releasing pain. Goodheart argues that different emotions can be released through different cathartic processes and she reminds us that emotion means 'to move'. We are 'designed' to move pain out of our bodies.

The pain can be released in different ways depending on the type of emotion we are dealing with:

☺ Laughter helps the release of fear and anger.

☺ Tears release fear and grief.

☺ Shaking releases fear.

If we do not release the tension and pain in our bodies, we store it and dis-ease develops. We suppress dis-ease with drugs and do not address the root cause, emotions that have turned inwards and have not been released. A key point from Goodheart's theory is that we can use our natural physiological responses to effectively manage our emotions, if we learn the courage to listen to our bodies and trust that we have the means with which to maintain health and well-being within ourselves.

Laughter, in this view, does not come from happiness but from pain. As the pain is released through laughter, our attention is freed up to access what she considers the natural state of a balanced individual, the state of love for the self and for others. She does not distinguish negative from positive emotions; all emotions are useful and are needed. Health comes from the re-balancing process being allowed to happen naturally. Ill health comes from stored-up emotions that have not been released through catharsis.

Whilst I share Goodheart's view that some laughter stems from pain, I believe that not all laughter does. Some laughter is an expression of happiness and joy. Not all laughter is the release of stored-up emotion. Her theory can be understood as indicating that laughter removes pain and allows us to feel happiness, and I can agree with this interpretation. I also believe that we continue to laugh to express joy in the absence of pain. In either case, laughter is always useful in maintaining our health.

Laughter and crying are the ways in which we re-balance our bodies and the site of both in the brain is the same. We can laugh until we cry, and we can also find ourselves in laughter after sobbing for a long period of time. The two processes are not that independent, nor should they be if they are a means of achieving the same thing: the release of emotion. It is therefore entirely appropriate to find laughter and tears in the experience of a loved one dying as well as in that of a loved one getting married.

G-MODE AND PLEASANT SHIFTS

John Morreal argues that there are three features in the approaches to laughter that we have discussed:

☺ There is a change in the psychological state of the laugher, which may be cognitive (as in the incongruity and superiority approaches) or affective (as in the emotional release approaches).

☺ The change must be sudden and not smooth; we can talk about this as a psychological shift.

☺ The shift must be pleasant. This is the case when we enjoy self-glory in the superiority approach, or amuse ourselves by the perception of some incongruity, or by experiencing release from pent-up emotion. We experience these shifts as good, and laughter is the indicator of that pleasure.

Morreal does not believe that pain causes laughter. He argues that laughter is the indicator of pleasure that we perceive as we release a painful emotion. For him, laughter is not the actual release of that emotion. To some extent this is too subtle a point for our purposes. We can assume that laughter happens as that release happens, and can leave the experts to argue about the detailed causal links.

The notion of a pleasant psychological shift is useful for our purposes. In babies, laughter happens as they perceive merely a shift in sensory input. As they grow older children become capable of perceiving conceptual or cognitive shifts. Emotional shifts are also part of this picture and though they have a cognitive component what leads to laughter is the shift between one emotional state, such as fear, and another such as relaxed security. So the notion of a psychological shift can explain in a more general way why we laugh.

An interesting aspect of Morreal's theory is that he does not view laughter as only the product of a feeling of security (the pleasant shift). He argues for there being a two-way causal link in which our behaviour (laughter) causes certain emotions. Thus, we can be happy because we laugh. He views the situation as a loop that we can break into either through the emotion or through the laughter. In this way, we can incorporate the idea that as we laugh we affect our emotions. One way of affecting these emotions is through releasing surplus emotional energy and another way is through creating a different emotion such as pleasure.

An even more general way of making sense of these different theories is to connect all that has gone on in this section with our understanding of the way people think. The psychological shift may simply be the shift from G-mode to D-mode, and laughter happens as we become consciously aware of that which we knew in our cognitive unconscious. This new consciousness can be of a sensory, cognitive or emotive nature. As we increase our awareness of what we know in a tacit way we gain greater control over our environment. Laughter can then be said to be an indicator of new conscious learning. Laughter helps us connect with our cognitive unconscious, or G-mode thinking.

It is this mode of thinking that will help us develop life below our necks. Laughter is our response to perceiving something anew. When we look at creativity, in chapter 5, we will connect this idea with our ability to find creativity in our everyday life. Associating non-habitual realms is a core skill of creative thinking. We need to become emotionally literate in order to be able to connect non-habitual realms. Emotional understanding is a prerequisite for thinking in both G-mode and D-mode.

EXPRESS YOUR EMOTICONS

Before moving on to explore how laughter can help you develop your emotional literacy, I want to take a tour into the world of e-mail and chat rooms – the world of electronic talk.

Firstly let's talk about live emotional talk. Have you any idea of the many words that we use to describe our emotional life? I have constructed below some tables to give you an idea. The answer to the question 'How are you feeling today?' can be the simple statement 'Fine, thank you' or it can take the form of a very rich description using many words from the tables below and more that the tables do not contain. However you choose to answer the question, people you are talking to can see you and from the non-verbal message will pick up how you are feeling even if you are just talking about the weather and not using any emotional language. They will have certain information coming to their senses that will help them generalise as to your overall emotional state. Check out the list below and feel free to add your own:

HOW ARE YOU FEELING TODAY?

Happy	Sad	Angry	Confused
Excited	Dissatisfied	Annoyed	Baffled
Blissful	Awful	Cross	Bewildered
Alive	Lonely	Grumpy	Harassed
Bubbly	Down	Irritated	Mixed up
Wonderful	Dreary	Indignant	Lost
Thrilled	Gloomy	Livid	Misunderstood
Lovely	Unwanted	Furious	Muddled
Proud	Hopeless	Outraged	Puzzled
Stupendous	Fed-up	Aggressive	Distraught
Elated	Grumpy	Seething	Unsure
Joyful	Miserable	Hostile	Hazy
Good	Sorry	Hateful	Unclear
Glad	Low	Enraged	Perplexed
Light	Deflated	Bad-tempered	Flustered

HOW ARE YOU FEELING TODAY?

Scared	Weak	Affectionate	Strong
Frightened	Apathetic	Loving	Able
Fearful	Worn-out	Warm	Active
Anxious	Useless	Caring	Confident
Apprehensive	Passive	Empathetic	Full of strength

Scared	Weak	Affectionate	Strong
Panicky	Impotent	Sympathetic	Determined
Threatened	Inferior	Ecstatic	Eager
Stunned	Fragile	Friendly	Firm
Petrified	Exposed	Fond	Forceful
Nervous	Disabled	Passionate	Capable
Worried	Deficient	Adoring	Bold
Jumpy	Defenceless	Tender	Assured
Insecure	Pathetic	Full of desire	Assertive
Terrified	Feeble	Connected	Courageous
Horrified	Unable	Delighted	Powerful

Some answers to the question have to do with how your body feels, rather than high-level descriptions of many body states:

Just to do with your body

Hot Cold Thirsty Sexy Shivery Ill Drunk Sweaty Dry Tired Exhausted Hurt Relaxed Fidgety Headachy Nauseous Tense Shaky Restless Twitchy Energised Grounded Solid Strong Weak Sickly Tight Loose

And there are some words that only have to do with laughter:

Just to do with laughter[24]

Caricature Mockery Pantomime Clowning Joke Prank Slapstick Sarcasm Buffoonery Satiric teasing

Farce Irony Jest Wit Parody Burlesque Gallows humour Ridiculousness Hoax Larking about Tomfoolery Repartee Whimsy Banter Lampooning Jocularity Amusement

We can use these words in conversation, and because they are accompanied by the non-verbal message, our emotions are conveyed to the other. These are arbitrary language signs and each points to a physical non-verbal experience. So it is relatively easy to decide on the meaning.

But what happens when humans are faced with a situation in which they cannot use their senses to gauge the meaning of the words? Some cynical reader might say, at this point, 'Good, we can get down to the task and purpose of the conversation and not get distracted by any of this touchy-feely stuff.' This is indeed how some businesses use e-mail. It is a medium of communication used to achieve a task, devoid of emotion. And when used as such it fails to be successful. People at work are complaining more and more about the miscommunication that happens with e-mail and how relationships suffer as the focus is only on task and information.

The situation is very different, you may already have found, with your teenage daughter. She loves e-mail. She comes home from school and 'gets on line' to her friends in a shared virtual chat-room – spaces in the computer where they can send e-mail to each other in real time and have virtual conversations. No complaints here, except perhaps from you.

People who use e-mail as a real tool for communication have not dispensed with the need to express emotions. They have created a new language that allows them to compensate for what the computer lacks – the possibility for perceiving the non-verbal message that accompanies our words. We have such a high need to express our emotions that we must get around this shortcoming if the medium is to work well for us. This new language has several components. For me they are an example of the never-ending ingenuity of human beings. Faced with a constraint we find creative ways around it.

The first component is called emoticons. No, not a word misspellt. Emoticons are little characters made up from different characters on the keyboard that are used to express the emotional tone of a given sentence on e-mail. E-mail does not easily handle pictures so the solution had to be found within the realm of what the keyboard could achieve. Also it had to be typed in quickly for real time conversation.

So here is how it works. You type your sentence and add the emoticons to mark the written page with the emotional tone of the message. Find below a small selection of the symbols that are being used by teenagers around the world. Notice the general pattern and learn to create your own. They are certainly an exercise in creative thinking. And, to me, also an example that human creativity is at its best when expected to perform within constraints. A clue if you are not familiar with this way of talking: Emoticons are written horizontally, but sometimes must be mentally turned to a vertical position to be understood.

So in answer to the question 'How are you today?' I may say ' 'Having a great time :o(just thought that I would sleep today #) ... today is a 80 day'. Or a message I got the other day from a friend,

Date: 16/06/99 20:47:01 GMT
From: Paul @ mike-home.freeserve.co.uk
To: laughingms@aol.com
( )
: _ *
: -)

<!DOCTYPE HTML PUBLIC "-//W3C//DTD W3 HTML//EN">

Here is the table I made up. Have fun working the emoticons out.

EMOTICONS

Symbol	Meaning	Symbol	Meaning
:-D	Big grin	:-P	Sticking out tongue
%-)	Confused	:-/	Perplexed
:P~~~	Drooling	;-)	Winking
:-$	Money where your mouth is	=:O	Frightened
:-o	Astonished	:-}	Embarrassed
;-^)	Tongue in cheek	[:-l]	Robot
8-0	Dazed	{:	Chuckie from Rugrats
;-j	Sarcastic	O:)	Angel
>:->	Devil	:()	Motor Mouth
:c	Very upset	: .)	Cyndy Crawford
:-D	Laughing	:o)	Smiley
( ) or { }	Hugs	:-@	Screaming/Angry
#-)	What a night!	B:-)	Wears sunglasses on head
:-T	Tight lipped	:'-(	Crying
[:-)	Wearing walkman!	3:-o	A cow
(l-l F	Robocop	:-[	Annoyed
:l	Frowing	~:)	A baby
*	Kiss	:-x	Kiss
:*(	Crying	:-(	Sad
:'-)	Happy tears	:?	Confused
:-#)	Smiley with moustache	Cl:-=	Charlie Chaplin
:-x	My lips are sealed	l-o	Bored

An interesting aspect of emoticons is that they provide a new level of communication for the written word. They are born out of the need to express emotion and to do it as quickly as one might be able to when talking face to face.

The second component I want to explore about this new language is the use of acronyms. Again to make virtual talk be like live talk it is necessary to type fast. This has led to developing shorthand for commonly used phrases but also for emotional expression. Have a read of the table below:

ACRONYMS

Symbol	Meaning	Symbol	Meaning
BG	Big grin	BTW	By the way
<G>	Grin	>GA	Go ahead
LOL	Laughing out loud	OTOH	On the other hand
TIA	Thanks in advance	WTG	Way to go
FAQ	Frequently asked questions	IMO	In my opinion
RTFM	Read the manual	BTW	By the way
PMFJI	Pardon me for jumping in	ROTFL	Rolling on the floor laughing
FWIW	For what it's worth	IMHO	In my humble opinion

So you can combine emoticons and acronyms to express yourself emotionally quickly on line. But there is yet another component to on-line talk. It is called geekcode, and it is designed to replace the implicit context of live conversation.

When we meet people, we make many assumptions about their lifestyle and their background just from first impressions. This is not possible with virtual talk and yet it is essential to our ability to communicate. We want people to know our preferences, what we like or what we don't like and the intensity with which we like or dislike something. Geekcode was designed to give virtual talk the tool with which to do this part of live conversation.

It works by assigning a series of plus and minus signs and other wild cards to the first letter of a given category. So you might say 'TV+++++' to indicate that you love television. Or you might say '!TV' to indicate that television is viewed with such contempt by you that you don't even own one. There are many categories that are common to the code but you can of course make your own. What you need to understand is the symbols for indicating the intensity ratings, that is, the symbols that express your emotional approach to the particular category. Here is a simple table to give you some examples:

GEEKCODE INTENSITY RATINGS[25]

Symbol	Meaning	Category	Example
----	I absolutely hate	Television	TV----
---	I hate	The X-files	X---
--	I dislike	Relationship	R--
-	I am ambivalent	Relationship	R-
	Neutral	Housing	H
+	I am positively ambivalent	Star Trek	T+
++	I like	Role playing	R++
+++	I love	Sex	Z+++
++++	I absolutely love	Doom – the game	D++++

The idea here is that you construct a portrait of yourself in geekcode to let others know about you. An example I particularly like is:

'!z+' which meant : **'Sex? What's that? No experience; willing to learn!'**

Your signature code might look something like this:

------BEGIN GEEKCODE BLOCK------

Version: 3.1

GED/J d-- s:++: a-- C++(++++) ULU++ P+ L++ E---- W+(-)
N+++ o+ K+++ w---O- M+ V-- PS++$ PE++$ Y++ PGP++ t-
5+++ X++ R+++$ tv+ b+ DI+++ D+++G+++++ e++ h r-- y++**

------END GEEKCODE BLOCK------

The code makes up a language that is very different from Standard English. Do visit the site *www.geekcode.com* to get the complete code and many examples. I am fascinated by the complexity of the code to express emotion. The intensity ratings give it a scale that can allow users to express many more things than simple likes or dislikes. The power of the arbitrary sign and our ability to assign meaning to any sign is truly one of the gifts of humanity.

I believe that the components of virtual talk deserve serious and fun study. Virtual talk is to me an example of how deep our need to express emotion is. We will find a way to express emotion even in a medium that does not easily lend itself to it. I also wonder if our children in having to learn to label their emotions in this way are developing their emotional literacy to levels that are higher than past generations which relied on the interpretation of emotion through the non-verbal channel.

I hope you have fun learning more about virtual talk. Visit *www.about.com* and search on emoticons. You will find a huge array of symbols that is growing daily. Or better still, design your own.

Let's now look at how laughter can help us learn to become more emotionally literate, more able to express our emoticons in real talk. A point that may not be obvious is that before being able to label my emotions I need to know what I'm feeling below the neck. And D-mode is not always aware of life below the neck. This is what developing our emotional literacy entails and is what I believe the younger generations are learning to do through virtual talk.

DEVELOPING OUR EMOTIONAL LITERACY

The chemicals that are running our bodies and our brains are the same chemicals that are involved in emotion. And that says to me that we had better pay more attention to our emotions with respect to health. Candace Pert

Each of the theories of laughter I have told you about is able to explain some types of laughter, but I doubt if any of them can satisfactorily explain every type of laughter. Superiority theories account very well for our laughter at small misfortunes and for the appeal of satire, but are less happy in dealing with word play, incongruity, nonsense, and indecency. Incongruity theories, on the other hand, are strong where superiority theories are weakest, and weak where they are strongest. Release theories account admirably for laughter at indecency, malice, and nonsense but are forced to concede that there is an intrinsic appeal in incongruity and word play that is quite independent of relief from restraint. Each type of theory does, however, illuminate some aspect of laughter. We spoke of a more general description being that of the pleasant psychological shift or, even more generally, that laughter was a human response to a new perception. Emotion is a fundamental part of our perception; the emotional evaluation of what we perceive is an integral part of our cognition.

Emotion is, therefore, our intelligence and we need to develop a language to describe it. G-mode is the language of our body. D-mode is the language of our mind. If, as Candace Pert suggests, the neuropeptides flowing through our bodies are our emotional intelligence, then we can no longer talk about the brain as being in the driving seat. We are our bodies and not just a brain. Laughter helps us make this body-mind connection.

> *I laughed, which Norman Cousins calls internal jogging,*
> *an exercise to keep us in emotional shape. I played. I let*
> *the emotions – and the peptides – flow.* Candace Pert

It is interesting that, though Pert says nothing much explicitly about laughter in her book,[26] she starts all her presentations with a funny cartoon to get her audience laughing. This is her way of connecting the body-mind and creating an audience that is present and engaged in the lecture she is about to give. I want to suggest to you the idea that laughter helps the flux of these neuropeptides. From this perspective it does not matter what emotion laughter can be directly associated with. What matters is that we laugh in order to free up the channels of communication.

> *I believe that happiness is what we feel when our*
> *biochemicals of emotions, the neuropeptides and their*
> *receptors, are open and flowing freely throughout the*
> *psychosomatic network, integrating and co-ordinating our*
> *systems, organs, and cells in a smooth rhythmic*
> *movement. Health and happiness are often mentioned in*
> *the same breath, and maybe this is why: Physiology and*
> *emotions are inseparable.*Candace Pert

Much of what we do in our busy lives supports a disconnection between the mind and the body. Psychoneuroimmunology research demonstrates that there are clear connections between our behaviour, our mental state and our physical being. Laughter enhances immune response. We feel less affected by stress if we perceive the world as a challenge and not a threat.

Laughter creates a connection between two realms, the physical and the mental, through our emotions. The link between the body and the mind is that of our emotional intelligence as represented by the communication of neuropeptides with all our key internal systems. Laughter helps us develop our emotional intelligence by connecting the physical and the conceptual through the emotional realm.

The more we laugh the more we can decrease the gap between what we know through our cognitive unconscious, G-mode, and what we know in consciousness. This is the tool that we need to develop to generate more conscious life below our necks. We do not want to be like the old joke of the head telling the body that the only reason why it kept the body was as a means of transport! Without our bodies we would know very little. It looks from current research that the whole body physically shares many of the properties we used to assign only to our brains until relatively recently.

Laughter helps us detach and not take life personally. This ability allows us to become more tolerant of inconsistency. As this ability develops within us, we lose the need to construct such a cohesive narrative of our behaviour from day to day. We are full of paradox and inconsistency and that is okay. It is not something to hide from others or ourselves. Our ability to do this makes us real and, in the terminology we have been using, allows G-mode patterns we are acting on to come to conscious D-mode – even when the patterns are ones that do not fit with the rational life narrative of D-mode. This is the junction of our being where development and growth can happen – the junction where integration of mind and body can happen daily, thus leading us to better health.

We have already said that most laughter is conversational[27] and not in response to humour. We must, therefore, focus our attention on increasing the kind of laughter that occurs naturally in conversation, as a means of helping our body remain healthy. In the next chapter we start to learn how to detach and not take life so seriously by learning to play with our pain respectfully.

CHAPTER 3

PLAYING WITH OUR PAIN:
PERMISSION TO LAUGH

You may think it odd for me to suggest that it is possible for us to play with our pain. When we are in the depth of pain, be it physical or emotional, we rarely see that we can choose to direct our attention in ways other than towards our suffering. And yet ...

> Here I lie. I have a tumour and you ask me where is my sense of humour. David Saltzman

Some people may consider this quote to be in bad taste. How can cancer be funny? There are those who found the concept of the film *La vita e bella* ('It's a beautiful life') difficult to grasp. Many comparisons were made of Roberto Benigni with Charlie Chaplin when the film won an Oscar for Best Foreign Film. *La vita e bella* encapsulates the message I want to convey. Find it on video and watch it if you can. A family in a concentration camp in Germany discovers that survival depends on their ability to put a frame of play around what happens to them every day. More specifically, a father helps his child cope with a terrible situation by convincing the child that they are participating in a game. The child wants to win the wonderful prizes and agrees to play.

When the film was released in England people commented, 'How can you make comedy about concentration camps?' To my mind those who viewed the film in this way missed the point. The film had a lot of laughter, yes. But was it a comedy? It was a film about how the way in which we choose to view what happens to us in our lives can make the difference between life and death. But for those of us leading 'normal' lives, our perspective 'only' makes the difference between thriving and surviving. We can choose to shut out our emotions in the hope of avoiding pain, or to let pain in and use our gift of laughter to make it bearable.

There was a lot of laughter in the film and there were also a lot of tears. The film was for me an emotional roller-coaster that taught me, better than anything I have ever read or seen, the most important skill in the art of living: We must be able to hold both our pain and our joy simultaneously when viewing our life experiences. The paradox of life is that everything that happens to us contains laughter and tears, like the symbol of the Tree of Life in Mexico that is divided in two halves, with one half representing death and the other representing life. The day of the dead in Mexico is a celebration of death in life.

When my husband and I were told by the hospital consultant that he only had a few days to live, we found our inner laughing place. We were told, in answer to my question of whether we got to go home in an ambulance, that the National Health Service could not afford it! We had a great laugh about the fact that I would not get to realise my ambition to go through London in half the time with the sirens ringing. Five minutes later I was alone in my car crying my eyes out, as he was being driven home in a hospital car without the siren. Both are true – the pain and the laughter. And if we view laughter as a way of re-balancing our body chemistry and getting those peptides talking to those receptors, then both are true *simultaneously* in the physical world too.

Seriousness does not stop because we laugh and funniness does not stop because we cry. They co-exist in our life and we must give ourselves permission to access both when we need to. Instead, we run to the doctor when we feel discomfort and get our choice of mood-altering drugs. These drugs make the promise of letting us have life on a good day every day. Doctors seduce us into believing that it is possible to have only half of the tree of life. As we pretend that it is possible to avoid our pain and those emotions that we would rather not have to go through, like grief and fear, we choose a different kind of pain, the kind of pain that makes us lose contact with parts of ourselves and leads to ill-health.

*As a culture we keep our feelings hidden, afraid to
express them honestly for fear others will be indifferent to
our sorrows or alienated or hurt by our anger. Better to
deny feelings, to suppress them, we tell ourselves, go
through the motions of happiness and pretend to have
fun – until the bottom falls out and the family physician
hands us the diagnosis: Depression.* Candace Pert

Pert refers to this as unhealed emotion, and argues that it is at the
core of many health problems we experience. We do not get to
choose if we want pain in our lives. The only thing that we get to
choose is what kind of pain we want; and whether we access that
inner laughing place to help us get our emotional life back in
balance.

*When you get to the end of your rope, tie a knot and
hang on. And Swing!* Leo Buscaglia

To the extent that we are willing to open up to our pain we can
experience joy. We either have access to all our emotions or we cut
ourselves off from them. Once you allow yourself to open up
emotionally you can experience life in all its richness. Not all of that
richness is pleasant but it is all necessary.

A long time ago Kahlil Gibran said this much more beautifully than
I ever could:

*Your joy is your sorrow unmasked. And the selfsame well
from which your laughter rises was oftentimes filled with
your tears. And how else can it be? The deeper that
sorrow carves into your being, the more joy it can contain.*

The new findings of psychoneuroimmunology, which we reviewed
in the last chapter, support the notion that all emotions have a
common physical substrate, the neuropeptides. Maybe, just
maybe, the peptide receptors are the well.

The film *La vita e bella* ends with the little boy saying to his mum:
'We won, mum, we won!' I found myself thinking: '… but it wasn't

a game' and almost immediately again: '… oh, but it was.' And both were true. Giving ourselves permission to laugh is about understanding this with all of our being. It may just be that until we have experienced the kind of pain that leaves nothing open to us but laughter, we will still have doubts about the appropriateness of playing with our pain to find laughter in our life. This is all part of our development as human beings and, sometimes, just knowing that it is possible may be enough to help us in difficult times. As the son of one of the participants in my laughter workshops said during his dad's funeral, 'I cannot find my laughing place yet, but knowing that it is there helps.'

And he turned to his people and said dry your eyes, we've been blessed and we are thankful. Raise your voices to the sky. This is a good day to die. Robbie Robinson

I learn an immense amount about my fears and myself when I play to myself the quote above and think of each day as a good day to die. To the extent I can truly believe this, I find laughter in my day. To the extent that I cannot, I find lots of tasks to do and feel disconnected from those around me. Stephen Levine wrote a book titled *A year to live.* In it he tells of his experiment to have his New Year resolution be to live that coming year as if it were his last. His is a way other than laughter of achieving the one result that seems to make the difference to our health: to be present in our life. Or as the title of a book I once saw: 'Relax, you may only have a few minutes left!' or another thought I find even funnier:

Don't take life too seriously – you will never get out of it alive!

An activity that may help you learn this skill of finding both pain and play in life events is set out below. This activity is also the basis for the more advanced techniques to come in the chapters that follow. I encourage you to understand and practise it every day for at least two weeks, before making a decision as to its usefulness and before moving on to learn from the chapters that follow.

Frame Shifting Activity[1]

In order to laugh we need the ability to shift our frame of reference at will. This simple exercise can teach us that we can do that easily and that personal change can happen as easily. All we need do is allow ourselves to shift our attention to different aspects of our experience.

This activity is in two parts and involves you talking about a memorable experience!

- Talk to a friend about your experience and filter it through the following frame of reference in your mind's eye:

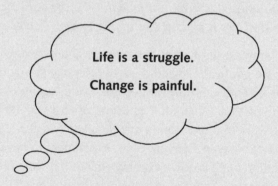

Life is a struggle.

Change is painful.

- Continue chatting with your friend, but now filter the *same* experience through a new frame of reference:

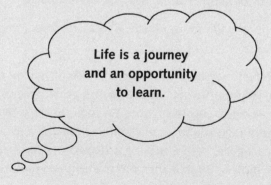

Life is a journey and an opportunity to learn.

Notice the differences you experienced in talking about the same content, but shifting frames of reference in your mind. Each time you do this, you experience the essence of what it means to change your mind. We shift our attention to a different aspect of our experience, one that was there all the time but to which we were not attending. The frames we put around our experience determine what aspect of it we pick out as being important, and I want you to be clear about one key component of the frame-shifting process: we can always choose our frames. And we often do not because we accept as given the frames of reference into which we are socialised. One of these frames, which permeate our culture, is that life should be a struggle and should be difficult. The notion of life as play and fun does not fit very well within our Protestant work ethic. And yet viewing life as play has many advantages when we think about our well-being.

THE POWER OF PLAY

Let's talk some more about the notion of play and its power to heal. When we joke about the misfortune of other people, and find the kind of laughter that superiority theories allude to, we allow ourselves to laugh at a victim. The victim is not real, but virtual. We say 'It's just a joke' and this means, it is not real. We are putting a play frame around something painful, as in the case of jokes about national tragedies. William Fry actually defines humour as play. 'First, humour is play. Cues are given that this, which is about to unfold, is not real. There is a "play frame" created around the episode.' From this we could argue that there is no hurtful humour. If we put a 'play frame' around it, any topic can be used to help us laugh.

To some extent this is true. But there is one crucial point missing from this interpretation. We must have permission to put a play frame around a topic, in order to avoid creating hurtful laughter. When we laugh at stereotypes or ethnic groups, we are putting a play frame around a topic without permission. This leaves us with the grey area: What happens when a member of a particular group laughs at his or her own group stereotype? I would say this is still hurtful laughter. The fact that I am Italian does not mean that I have permission from all Italians to make jokes about the stereotypical traits of Italians.

A good practical model to help us decide when laughter is hurtful and when it is healing is to use Charlie Chaplin as a benchmark. He is quoted as saying: 'To truly laugh, you must be able to take your pain and play with it.' We can call this Chaplin's equation. And it is this that we see him do in all his work. There are two aspects of this approach that I want to highlight to you. Firstly, he does not talk about the pain of others, but of his own pain. Secondly, a hallmark of his work is that he plays with human pain with heaps and heaps of compassion. It is the same quality that I see in Roberto Benigni. When we explored, in chapter 1, the ways in which we learn, we defined play as an activity that is done for its inherent value. I believe this to be significant. There is no ulterior motive in true play, and it is this quality that we must strive for in our pursuit of *levitas*.

True play can *only* be healing. In true play there is a lot of laughter that is of the conversational kind and not of the humour kind. Its power comes from the fact that it stops us from what Mathias Alexander calls 'end-gaining', the carrying out of an activity without attention to the process of the activity. He refers to the process as the 'means-whereby' we achieve a goal. He argues that it is our inability to stop end-gaining that leads to our body functioning in a sub-optimal way. To grasp in a second the power of true play we need only watch children. It is no surprise that within the Alexander Technique, the technique that Mathias developed for relearning how to use our body, children are often used as an example of effortless body use – something that, with all our end gaining, we lose as adults and have to re-learn to avoid back injury.

So we must play with our pain with compassion and permission. This gives us control over the means whereby we achieve our ends. It allows us to make a choice to laugh or cry in any situation. It teaches us that we have a certain kind of choice.

Next, to help you in your laughter education, I want to offer you some simple models to categorise what makes you laugh and help you decide if you are creating more pain and hurt for yourself or if you are healing yourself through your laughter. Know that whatever you are currently doing you are doing for a purpose and that you can always make different choices if better options become available.

AM I HURTFUL OR AM I HEALING?

Laughter has a dark side to it. We are so starved of emotional connection that we cause pain to ourselves and to others to find ways of laughing together. Teasing, ridicule and certain kinds of humour have this quality. They generate laughter at the expense of yourself, as when you put yourself down to get a laugh; or at the expense of others, as when you pick a particular ethnic group and through assigning negative qualities to it you have a good laugh at their expense. As I said before, this is laughter without permission and, often, without compassion.

So, what kind of laughter are you encouraging around you?

WHAT KIND OF LAUGHER ARE YOU?

I have already emphasised that my focus here is not humour, but as we get into discussing the kind of laughter that you are encouraging around you, I know of a simple model that may help you define your kind of laughter. It is adapted from a book by Ray Moody called *Laugh after laugh*. He describes five different types of humour, each with different aims. Do you recognise yourself in any of them? The categories he identified are fairly intuitive, but I have included an example of what a typical expression of each category would sound like if we were to blow the cover of what are normally covert psychological games.

Category	Typical expression	Aim
Common	'She thinks I'm funny. I have a sense of humour'	To find people who laugh at the same things I do
Conventional	'We think we are funny. We have a sense of humour'	To develop group cohesiveness, we belong to the same group
Good sport	'You do it to me. You have a sense of humour'	To cover up that I'm hurt by your comments, I laugh.
Life of the party	'I'm always funny. I have a sense of humour'	To keep control of my emotions and other people's by making them laugh.
Cosmic	'Life is funny. We can laugh'	I give myself permission to laugh and others can choose to join me.

We use all of these categories to different extents. Some are a protective device which allow us to cope with unresolved emotion, and as such we want to acknowledge their useful purpose. When we find laughter through the 'good sport' and 'life of the party' strategies we are not seeking permission; we are often creating more pain by laughing at what hurts us and are not using a true play frame. True play has no agenda, but with these strategies we do have a hidden agenda: We either want to control others or to maintain emotional distance from others. We are not fully engaged in the interaction. This may be appropriate to the situation or it may not. The key problem with both these strategies is that people do not get to fully choose if they want to participate. Permission is not asked for and is not given.

The 'common' and 'conventional' strategies meet our criterion for healing laughter: permission. The downside of these strategies is that they are other-dependent. I rely on others to find me funny, and can laugh only with their permission, that is if they laugh with me. This other-dependency is often present in the stereotype of the comedian that can only laugh with an audience. These strategies work as long as there are other people who choose to laugh with you.

The last strategy, the cosmic, is what I would describe as the prototype of healthy humour and laughter. We reflect on the paradox of life, and find laughter in the human condition as fully paid up members of it. There is permission, there is choice and there is no judgement of yourself or others. This is the kind of laughter that we find in those who are able to use laughter to heal themselves and others – as we will see below when we explore living theories of laughter.

EGO-STATES AND LAUGHTER

Another simple framework for you to describe your approach to laughter comes from an area of psychology known as transactional analysis (TA).[2]

Think of your mind as having different states available to it. You could identify times when your responses come from an adult state of mind (the Adult ego-state in TA) and this is when you respond from the reality of the present moment. You gather facts and data. At other times you may respond as if you were a parent talking to a child (the Parent ego-state in TA). Here you are responding in your interaction from the rules and regulations that you have generalised from your parents and other authority figures in your life. You evaluate positively or negatively. A last state of mind that you may easily identify is when you behave as a child might (the Child ego-state in TA). You act emotionally and can be playful.

These ego-states (Parent, Adult, and Child) can be further divided and become very complex diagrams to help us understand people. Do read a book on TA if you are interested in the wider theory. We are only touching the surface here. What I offer you below is a simplified table, using the TA model, to explore where healthy laughter lies.

Ego-state	Healthy/unhealthy laughter	Comments
Parent, further divided into: Critical parent, Nurturing parent	Unhealthy. Laughing at people's failings when it comes from the critical parent.	As we are working with evaluation, the kind of laughter that this ego-state elicits tends to put people down, through control or dependency.
Adult	Neutral	About data and facts. If there is laughter it will be about the situation rather than the person and likely to be healthy.
Child, further divided into: Free child, Adapted child, Little professor	Healthy at times. The little professor is said to be the source of creativity and wisdom. Viewed as the adult in the child. Has access to the emotions and also an ability to gather data accurately. Free child is the source of true play.	Certainty about emotions. At times we can behave as adapted children, following the rules. We laugh at what society says is funny. At other times we can behave as free children or as 'little professors'. It is here that we can find access to our cosmic sense of humour through true play.

The theory holds that everybody has these three ego-states available to a greater or lesser extent and that through practice we can develop those that we may have lost touch with. TA assumes that we have or can develop choice as to how we use them. The theory holds that when we want to find laughter in our lives we should encourage contexts and people around us who help us access our Free child and our Little professor. *Levitas* lies in the Child and *levitas* is important. We may do well to remember, as my colleague Joanne Garner has stated that the 'joker' is the most powerful card in the pack.

You can check in the table on page 70 some of the typical qualities of each ego-state and decide for yourself what your preferences are when you are trying to find laughter with others. I have not included the Adult ego-state, as laughter is not strongly associated with this state.

The kind of laughter I want you to develop and get in touch with is the kind that is associated to the Child ego-state. It is there that our capacity for true play lies and that our capacity for thinking creatively and feeding our exploratory drive can be found.

Muriel James and Dorothy Jongeward have written a book about TA, called *Born to win*,[3] and it stresses the importance of keeping our connection to our Child in order to find healthy laughter in our lives:

> *The person who cannot laugh or bring laughter to others, whether at age seven or seventy, is probably adapted to fear the potential intimacy that shared laughter is likely to bring. Shared laughter is also a way of being transparent, and some people always have their guards up.*

If you think about the way in which we structure our time with other people you could draw a continuum that looks like this:

Withdrawal → Rituals → Pastimes → Activities → Games → Intimacy[4]

TA suggests that the degree of risk which is connected with these different ways of interacting with each other, increases as we move towards intimacy. We are more likely to be rejected by the other if we choose to be transparent. Intimacy is set up between two adults and transparency is always part of the deal if it is to

	Critical parent	Nurturing parent
Sample words	You, bad, should, ought, must, always, ridiculous	Good, nice, I love you, I'll help you, wonderful, great!
Voice	Abnormal stress on sentences, marked words to indicate implied judgement	Abnormal stress, words are marked to imply 'I'll take care of you'
Gestures	Frowning, finger pointing, hard facial expression	Open arms, soft facial gestures, pat on the back
My fears	Loss of control	To be of no use to others
What I value	Order and security	Kindness and concern for others
Aim	To judge negatively persons I'm talking to and let them know they could do better	To judge positively persons I'm talking to and let them know that I'll take care of them
Kind of laughter	Life of the party	Conventional

Adapted Child	Free Child and Little Professor
Can't, please, May I?, Yes, I will, thank you. Do they like me?	Wow, fun, want, let's play, ouch, I love it, I wonder if ...
Quiet volume, monotone, compliant tone	High volume, high pitch and very changeable. Lots of exclamation marks
Body still, hand in mouth, eyes down, nodding	Hand and arm waving, jumping up and down, mark out emotions with whole body
To be rejected	To be bored
Being accepted and liked by others	Change, creativity and fun
To comply with the socialisation rules I have been taught, to rebel against these same rules	To have fun, to find out and to imagine possibilities. To have my own way at any cost
Common and good sport	Cosmic

work. There is reciprocity and openness. This may give you a clue as to what happens in your relationships when you find yourself in laughter with some people but not with others. Laughter brings us together and I may not want to have that level of transparency with everyone I meet! With some people I may just choose to stick to a ritual: 'Good Morning, how are you?' 'I'm fine. Thank you. How are you?' 'Very well'. Not much potential for laughter there, don't you think?

I have included below three activities to help you re-connect with your Child. If you are one of those people who have lost touch with your Child, you will have lost touch with your ability to use your senses fully, to experience the world in as full a way as is possible. G-mode thinking is developed through increased sensory awareness of the present and we explored earlier its value in helping us deal with a complex world.

The activities are adapted from *Born to win* and I have chosen them to help you develop your connection with that part of you that will allow healing rather than hurtful laughter to find you more often in your daily life.

Developing a connection with your Child: Activity 1

☺ Find yourself a place where you can be comfortable, outside or inside, and choose an object to focus on as if you had never seen it before in your life. Do this for a few minutes, and then de-focus from the object and allow the background to come into focus.

☺ Focus on your hearing now. Listen out for sounds outside of you. What can you hear? What sounds are near? What sounds are far away? Do you notice sounds that are constant?

☺ Now turn your attention to what you can smell. Notice the air going through your nostrils. What smells do you recognise?

☺ And as you let go of noticing and recognising smells you can allow yourself to direct your attention to what you can taste. What is the quality of the tastes in your mouth? What texture does your tongue have as you explore your mouth with it?

☺ Now allow yourself to notice how the surface of your skin feels. What do you notice first? What temperature is your skin? Warm, hot, cold? Does it feel different in different parts of your body? Or does it feel the same?

☺ Developing your sensory awareness engages you in the present and helps you notice how you feel. It is here that you can connect with your laughter and your emotions. Practise this exercise daily and use it to take your emotional temperature. We could call this activity the emotional thermometer!

Developing a connection with your Child: Activity 2[5]

Think about what you enjoyed as a child. Choose something that is all right to do but that you have not done in a very long time and find a way to do it again now.

☺ Watch the clouds: find a comfy spot to decipher cloud pictures. Find a friend to do it with!

☺ Walk in the rain: without shoes or an umbrella; jump into those puddles!

☺ Be a cat: curl up in the sun and enjoy the feeling of it on your skin.

☺ Climb a tree: head to the nearest tree and look at the view from above.

☺ Fly a kite. Play with a pet. Eat an ice cream.

☺ 'Like a child, have fun. Enjoy yourself. Winners do.'

Developing a connection with your Child: Activity 3

Some of us have access to play in our lives. For some it is a major focus in what they choose to do; for others less. Reflect on how it is for you.

☺ Do you have enough play in your life right now?

☺ What are your favourite ways to play?

☺ Is playing an important part of your life or do you think it is wasteful and unproductive?

☺ Where and with whom do you like to play? Are you an active or a passive player?

☺ Write an advertisement for the perfect playing partner.

☺ If you need some help to imagine yourself playing at all: Direct a movie, in the comfort of your own mind, of you playing a favourite game. See, hear, feel yourself there. Allow yourself in your imagination to smile, laugh, shout, jump up and down, have as much fun as you dare ... after all, it's not for real!

I'd like to end this section on healing laughter by asking you to reflect on the fact that healing seems to come from our connection with our origins, that which made us unique and special before we took on all the socialisation messages that allow us to be part of our society as we develop into adulthood. We would not want to be without those aspects of ourselves which enable us to function in our communities and be part of social groupings. Equally we should not be without that which is the hallmark of our uniqueness. We heal ourselves and others to the extent that we are able to connect with others in shared laughter, and we can only do that if we allow others to share with us in true play.

> We shall not cease from exploration, and the end of all our exploring will be to arrive where we started and know the place for the first time. TS Elliot

THE EMOTIONAL CYCLE

As we learn to re-connect with our laughter and to play with our pain with permission and compassion, we need to know more about how we process our emotions. Some ways of dealing with our emotions are healthy and others can lead us to the condition which Candace Pert calls unhealed feeling or emotion. Unhealed feelings lead to physical illness.

We can look at our emotional process as going through two interconnected cycles. One I call the reality cycle, because it leads us to having free attention to sense the world in the present moment. The other I call the magical thinking cycle, because it leads further and further away from sensing the present moment.

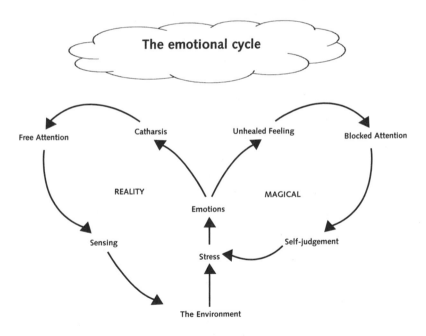

Our starting point is the internal stress that is generated by what happen to us in the external environment. The stress and tension of our daily lives has an impact on our bodies. At a physical level, neuropeptides communicate within and between the different systems of our body to enable the right actions to happen to maintain our health. At a psychological level we experience different sensations and label them as emotions.

We experience about eight primary emotions: sadness, disgust, anger, anticipation, joy, acceptance, fear and surprise. Using the analogy of colours, these can be mixed to get other secondary emotions. Joy and fear make up guilt. Fear and surprise make up alarm. Self-judgement is made up of anger and disgust.[6] We can also distinguish between emotion, mood and temperament, the significant parameter in this distinction being duration. Emotions are transient, mood may persist over a number of days, and temperament is understood to be stable over time. The primary emotional components do not change even if the duration does. I use the term emotion here to refer to all that I have just explained as well as the basic sensations of pleasure and pain, and also basic drives like hunger, thirst and the exploratory drive that I referred to in relation to play.[7]

> Let me begin by saying that I believe all emotions are healthy, because emotions are what unite the mind and the body. Anger, fear and sadness, the so-called negative emotions, are as healthy as peace, courage and joy. To repress these emotions and not let them flow freely is to set up a dis-integrity in the system, causing it to act at cross-purposes rather than as a unified whole. The stress this creates, which takes the form of blockages and insufficient flow of peptides signals to maintain function at the cellular level, is what sets up weakened conditions that can lead to disease. The key is to express it [the emotion] and let it go, so that it doesn't fester or build, or escalate out of control. Candace Pert

As we experience emotions we choose to follow either the healthy reality cycle, or the unhealthy magical cycle. If we follow the reality cycle, we move from the emotion to catharsis. We release the emotion and let it go. It is here that laughter plays its role in our health. We release emotions through laughter. According to some models, fear and anger are released through laughter. Other emotions are released through yawning, shaking, crying, and sweating. There are many theories, some of which we explored in the previous chapter, about how this process of catharsis happens. We do not yet know what the actual connections are between each specific emotion and how its release is achieved. We do know that laughter is a cathartic process and that certain emotions are released though it. We also know that laughter, through changes in breathing, can alter neuropeptide activity in the body. As we use laughter to release emotions, we are able to free up our attention to focus on the sensory experience of the present and we become able to perceive our environment more fully. We can therefore deal more effectively with new stimuli. This is how the healthy cycle seems to work.

The unhealthy cycle, the magical thinking cycle, also starts with the emotion we experience in response to the stress of the environment. We may, however, believe that it is not appropriate to release the emotion, or may not yet know how to release emotions safely. We store up these emotions in our bodies, and experience them as feelings that we carry as background to all that we do. These feelings become old feelings. As we hang on to them they become part of our identity; they become who we are in our interactions with others. I am depressed, for example. These unhealed feelings block the free flow of emotions and block my attention. They lead to an inability to engage with people in a full way. A simple example of this happened to me just this morning as I decided to book a taxi to take me to the airport in a couple of days. Here is the story.

My normal taxi company was unavailable and I remembered that there was another company I had used in the past. I looked for the number but could not find it in any of my address books. I thought it strange, but persevered. I found the number in the Yellow Pages, dialled it and recognised the woman who answered the phone:

Taxi Company (TC): For what time?

Mariana (MF): Ten in the morning

TC: The address?

MF: Essex Street in Horsham

TC: We have been there before.

MF: Yes, you have. I had lost your number so I haven't called you in a while ...

TC: We went to get you at the airport once and you did not turn up. Our driver waited for two hours. [angry voice] We don't take people like that again. It costs us money!

MF: [I then remembered why I had taken their number out of my book. My perception was that they had not turned up and that had cost *me* money and time] I was there and my perception had been that your driver had not turned up.

TC: Well, we did and waited for two hours! If you had been there you would have called us ...

MF: I will not argue with you. Thank you very much. Please forget about the booking.

I laughed as I put the phone down. The incident she was referring to had happened well over a year earlier and her anger was so present, so real. It was, for her, as if it had happened the day before. I, on the other hand, had simply made a choice not to use the company again and deleted the number from my address book. I completely forgot the incident, until I was on the receiving end of her anger. I then recalled the incident very vividly and chose not to respond in kind. Here is an example of the magical thinking cycle. This woman was hanging on to old anger about a particular incident in her life and lost sight of the fact that her behaviour on the phone cost her even more money and a customer!

This is an example of what happens to me if I do not have enough free attention to engage and attend to others because my attention is being used up by the unhealed feelings I hold in my body. It is as if I had 100 Scrunchies of attention to spend that I can only get back as I let go of the emotions I experience. If I have spent 80 on keeping old feelings, I cannot spend them on noticing the sounds around me right now. We go through life being attention poor, which can lead to an inability to interact successfully with the world and can create more stress.

The magical cycle continues as I increase my awareness that too much of my attention is being taken up by these blocked feelings. I develop a tendency to judge myself for not being able to feel 'normal'. I create more stress for myself through self-judgement. This cycle never connects back to the outside world. It is not about what is happening in my life right now. It's about the accumulation of unhealed feelings that I'm carrying around with me. It is because of this that I have called it magical thinking. It is not grounded in reality and yet can cause more and more pain as I hang on to my feelings and cannot find safe ways of releasing them.

It is that release that gives me back the Scrunchies that I can spend on paying attention to the outside world as I am perceiving it right now and not as it was ten years ago.

I need you to understand that I am not endorsing cathartic therapy as the only tool to get back to the healthy emotional cycle. I do not support any approach to developing ourselves emotionally that requires that we spend our lives hitting cushions or crying and laughing during many a therapy session to release all the emotions that we have stored up over the years we have been alive. There is, however, something that this type of approach *can* achieve. It can help us learn about the connection between our emotions and the processes we have available to release them. This was of great personal benefit to me when I was going through the process of grieving for my husband's death. I literally did not know how to express what I was feeling, in a safe way. Cathartic laughter therapy helped me forge new links between my behaviour and my emotions. I am not alone in having had to learn to make these new links.

Many of us simply do not know, or have forgotten, how to laugh or cry. The process is one of learning, of education. Cathartic therapy can help us relearn this connection, and laughter is one way of relearning how to play with our pain and stay in, or get back to, the reality cycle. Once the connection is made, however, we must move away from laughter as therapy. We need to learn how to safely release our emotions in our daily lives. The haven of the therapy room creates the false impression that it is the only safe place, that we can only release our emotions with our therapist. This is a recipe for dependency. I have experienced therapeutic relationships based on this dependency and they do not lead to emotional maturity.

There is a place for therapy in making the connection. There is also a place for lifeskills training to learn how to safely express our emotions as we go about the business of our daily lives, becoming self-sufficient and emotionally intelligent. Reconnecting with our conversational laughter is a good way to start on the road to emotional genius. Let's explore some key communication skills to help us laugh more away from the therapy room.

COMMUNICATION STRATEGIES FOR HEALING LAUGHTER

You now understand that laughter is a way to health, that healing laughter is about permission and compassion, about making contact with the part of you that can find ways of playing even with that which is painful. I do not want you to get the impression that laughter is an appropriate way for releasing any emotion. People come to my workshops and tell about their desire to learn to laugh 'because they are tired of crying'. Laughter does not replace other ways of releasing emotions. We need to do it all. Laughter can sometimes help us connect with our emotional well and we then realise that we have a lot of crying to do. The strategies that follow will increase your ability to laugh *if it is laughter your body needs*. According to Annette Goodheart, anger and fear can be released through laughter, but grief cannot be released in this way. Laughter is not a substitute for exploring all our emotions, and remember that you will be able to laugh only to the extent that you are able to cry.

I want to share with you some communication strategies I adapted from my work with Annette Goodheart that will help you develop your laughter quotient. Learn how to apply them to help yourself. Make them work for you before you involve other people in their use. It is easy to focus on getting others to laugh in order to divert your attention from what you actually need to attend to – helping yourself laugh more.

THE LAUGHTER QUESTIONS

Find a place and a time in your day where you can be undisturbed. You are going to take time out to visit your internal world. It is rare in our day-to-day lives that we allow ourselves to simply stop. We don't even know if we are breathing, though we assume we are, as we rush around from one task to the next. Your task right now is only to sit and notice what is going on in the comfort of your own mind. Once you have allowed yourself to just sit and notice for a few minutes, focus on the questions below to help you connect with your emotional self and find laughter in past situations that are still emotionally present for you:

☺ As I sit here noticing my breathing, what do I want to put my attention to?

☺ What is it in my life that I want to laugh about?

☺ What is not funny in my life that I would like to laugh about?

Allow yourself time to let into your consciousness a particular situation that you want to attend to. You may choose something specific or just allow something to emerge from your cognitive unconscious. Let the situation form in your mind's eye and as it forms you can hear those characteristic sounds and see the right kind of pictures and feel what you feel. Notice what is important for you about the situation. You can now move on to ask the following question:

☺ What sentence can remind me of this experience so that I can work with it?

Your aim here is to find a simple sentence you can play around with that can re-connect you with the experience you want to laugh about. Once you have that sentence, and you know for yourself that laughter is what this situation needs, you can move on to the following questions to help you play with it:

☺ This is not funny. Have I laughed about not laughing yet?

☺ This is not funny for me right now. How could it be funny?

☺ How can I help myself laugh about this situation right now?

☺ What will it take to make me laugh?

The aim of the questions above is to link laughter with the situation that had not been funny until now. Laughter comes from incongruity, as we saw in the previous chapter. As you connect two incongruous contexts, like laughter and pain, you can generate laughter for yourself. The laughter that you generate helps you release any emotions that you had stored up in your body in relation to that situation. You may choose to do this with a friend and ask him or her to listen to your story and ask you the questions. Their task is to *only* ask the questions and not to engage you in conversation. You want to get to laughter and laugh together without talking for as long as you can manage it.

Annette Goodheart also suggests that you can add 'tehee' to the end of your sentence, or 'hohoho', or 'hahaha'. This achieves the same result. The 'silliness' of putting these two items together gets you to laughter. I call this the 'Tehee Practice' in my workshops, and it is a very powerful and simple technique to find a way to our laughing place.

Another technique is the one I call 'Making things better by making them worse'. This technique is good for situations that may be coming up for you in the near future. It involves you taking a situation where you fear the worst might happen and asking yourself the following question as many times as it takes to get you to laughter:

☺ And if that happened, then what would happen?

When you start thinking about how bad you feel about this situation, and how unable to deal with it you are, take some pen and paper and write down your worst nightmare. Write for at least 10 minutes. The only rule is that you write nothing positive. Asking the question above will help you to get to the most ludicrous scenarios. If you are like most of us, by the time you have seen yourself doing that important presentation, say, with all your slides messed up, lying on the floor with a broken leg, reaching for a gun and shooting your audience, you may start seeing the funny side of things and you will be ready to get on with it.

Another strategy is the one I call 'Let's be serious'. When I am taking myself too seriously, or I'm up on my soap-box about something, I know this is not healthy for me or those around me. The game here consists of sitting down and getting really engrossed in the seriousness of the situation. It is as if I created a witness in my head to explore the seriousness.

As I observe myself in my mind's eye doing and saying what needs to be said and done, I write, or tell myself, just how serious it all really is. And the aim here is to be *really* serious. As you do this for a few minutes, you may find yourself starting to laugh. You may enlist the help of a friend to engage with you in the seriousness of it all until *you*, not your friend, start to laugh. The questions that can help you here are:

☺ This is very serious, isn't it?

☺ And just how serious do you think this is?

The final strategy that I want to offer you is called 'Finding your laughter category'. You will have certain key words that make you laugh. We all do. As you talk to others about your unfunny situation or think about it, you will find words that help you laugh. These are your laughter categories and it is good to know what they are so that you can repeat them and get yourself laughing more and more about the situation. We all have particular associations about our experiences. As we hear a particular song, we remember that old friend from university. As we smell coffee, we think of our childhood. This process is called anchoring and is a fundamental cognitive ability. It is the way in which we build connections in our knowledge network. Comedians use this a great deal. They keep repeating the gesture or word that is linked to laughter in the mind of the audience. For this strategy to work you need to attend to what triggered your laughter the first time you talked or thought about it. The questions here are:

☺ What is the one thing (sound, picture, feeling in your body) that will give me on-going access to laughter in this situation?

☺ What did I say, see or feel in my body just before I found myself laughing?

USEFUL FRAMES TO PUT AROUND PLAYING WITH OUR PAIN

I have summarised below the key underlying assumptions of the approach to playing with pain I have offered you in this chapter. It is important that you understand and use the strategies above, making the assumptions below, as this will ensure that you treat yourself and others with respect:

☺ As I am in charge of my emotions, so are other people.

☺ For laughter to heal, it must happen with permission from all parties involved.

☺ I and others can choose where to direct our attention.

☺ The laughter category is the filing tab for the experience.

☺ I and others may not be ready to laugh about the experience and that is okay.

☺ When using these strategies with others, I only ask questions for their information and not mine.

☺ I can remind myself that I can laugh.

☺ We seek laughter only, not conversation.

☺ We can only reorganise our experience if we know what our experience is. My initial task is to notice what is, not to change it.

☺ Crying and laughter serve a useful purpose in our well-being: they free up our attention to deal with the world.

I have offered you an approach to find more laughter in your life and deal with those situations that cause you pain and stress. We have explored the link between laughter, pain and play. I have offered you some ways in which you can learn to play with your pain in a respectful way. Drawing from the work of Annette Goodheart, Candace Pert and others I have offered you what I call my living theory of laughter. I have described the ways in which I use laughter in my life and the reasons why it plays such a fundamental part in my ability to develop my emotional intelligence.

I now want to move on to offer you a way in which you can learn more about your own living theory of laughter. Your aim in doing this work is to have an increased level of awareness of who you are and why you do what you do.

GUIDELINES TO DEVELOP YOUR OWN LIVING THEORY OF LAUGHTER

> *I work on the certainty that you have everything you need. It has only to be accessed.* Virginia Satir

In order for you to develop your ability to find laughter in your life, you need to pay attention to your own psychogeography, that is, the aspects within you which you bring to bear when you apply a given ability to the world.[8] I am suggesting that you have to spend time going through a process of exploring your psychogeography as a way of developing your ability to laugh more. The process below will give you a way to create a useful map of your own experience and behaviour.

This process will allow you to become more aware of just how you organise your experience in relation to laughter. You may find aspects to your living theory of laughter that you like, things you do or believe that actually help you laugh more. You may also find other aspects you do not like as much, such as beliefs that limit your ability to laugh. What you like, as well as what you do not like, however, counts as useful information in the light of increasing your awareness of your psychogeography. What you do not like you have the ability to change, but you cannot change it until you become aware of it.

FINDING YOUR OWN LIVING THEORY OF LAUGHTER: SOME GUIDELINES[9]

Here is the self-elicitation process. I suggest that you read it through once to familiarise yourself with the steps. Have available a writing pad to note down any insights or questions that emerge as you go on this strange walk. A piece of paper labelled 'My limiting beliefs' may also be of use to you. On this paper you can note down any statements that come to you of the form: 'I can't ...' 'I shouldn't ...' 'One should never ...' 'It is not right to ...' 'This is stupid and ...'.

These statements will be useful to you when, in the next chapter, we look at the beliefs we hold that can limit our ability to laugh. Just keep a record of them for now. You will have an opportunity to reorganise your beliefs if you so choose.

Enjoy your walk.

1. Physically lay out on the floor five pieces of paper with the following headings written on each: Ability, Action, Strategy, Beliefs and Emotions. Now get ready to take a strange walk. We will bring to the outside world that which you normally carry in the comfort of your own mind. You will be mapping out your mind as if you were organising furniture in a room, to allow you to see what is there when you are at your best. Lay out the map on a straight line on the floor and start walking.

2. Start your walk standing in the *Ability* space and ask yourself the following question:

   Q: 'What exactly am I able to do?' Your answer may be that you are able to laugh when you choose. Find a sentence that describes your ability in relation to laughter to your satisfaction.

3. Standing in the *Action* space, answer the question:

   Q: 'What am I doing on the outside when I demonstrate this ability?' To answer this question you have to see, and hear, and feel yourself laughing in the environment you choose. Create your own movie of you laughing in the context that is appropriate for you. Once you have the movie in your mind you are ready to continue your walk.

4. Standing in the *Strategy* space, answer these questions:

   Q: 'How do I know I am being successful?' The answer here is about the trigger in your internal world that lets you know you've got it right, that you are laughing in just the way that is appropriate for you and the context you are in. Your Test of success.

Q: 'What do I do to satisfy my success test? What do I do when my test is not sufficiently satisfied?' Find out what goes on in your mind in order to get to the point that you experience that trigger and also find out what you do when you try to get to the trigger and you are not able to. If you think of your mind as a machine, you can view this question as asking you about the operations that must be carried out in order to get to successful results. The other question asks you about the operations that must be carried out when the results you are getting are not what you want. Create your list of tests and operations and continue walking.

5. Standing in the *Beliefs* space now, answer these questions:

Q: 'When you laugh, what is important to you?' You will get a list of values, the criteria that make laughter important for you.

Q: 'What do you mean by each value?' You will get the experience that is associated with each value.

Q: 'What makes it possible for you to satisfy your values in the context of your ability to laugh?' The answer to this question will give you the enabling cause and effect link between each value and what makes each value possible in your theory.

Q: 'Why are the values important?' The answer to this question will give you the motivating cause-effect link, what the realisation of each value achieves for you. This cause and effect pattern is the structure of your beliefs about laughter. Move on.

6. Standing in the *Emotions* space, answer the question:

Q: 'When you laugh and satisfy your beliefs, what are you feeling that sustains and gives you feedback signals that it's working?' You are looking for the label you give to the emotion that supports you in carrying out this ability in the world. The label you choose should enable you to do the next step easily.

7. Experience that sustaining *emotion* now. Note the physiology and inner experience of it. What you are experiencing in your body as that emotion will be the core of your *ability*. You are now ready to retrace your steps. Go back into the *Beliefs* space so you experience both at the same time: your *beliefs* that support you in this *ability* and the *emotions* that sustain you. Notice how the *emotion* enriches your initial experience of the *Belief* space.

8. Take with you the experience of both your sustaining *emotion* and your *beliefs* and bring them into your *Strategy* space. Again notice how it enhances or enriches your initial experience of your laughter strategy.

9. Bring your sustaining *emotion*, your *beliefs* and your *strategies* into the *Action* space. Experience how strengthened and changed or enriched your actions can be with your increased conscious awareness of what supports you in laughter.

10. Bring your *emotions*, *beliefs*, *strategies* and *actions* into the *Ability* space. Notice how even the simplest actions are reflections and manifestations of all your psychogeography. All of who you are.

11. Bring all these levels of yourself into your next conversation with a friend and experience how it is transformed and enriched by your increased conscious awareness of all of you. Know that you can bring your *ability* to laugh to any situation you choose.

A STRUCTURE FOR OUR LIVING THEORY OF LAUGHTER

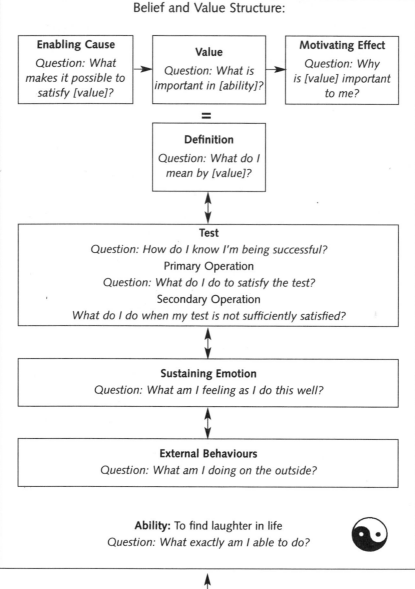

Belief and Value Structure:

Enabling Cause
Question: What makes it possible to satisfy [value]?

Value
Question: What is important in [ability]?

Motivating Effect
Question: Why is [value] important to me?

=

Definition
Question: What do I mean by [value]?

Test
Question: How do I know I'm being successful?
Primary Operation
Question: What do I do to satisfy the test?
Secondary Operation
What do I do when my test is not sufficiently satisfied?

Sustaining Emotion
Question: What am I feeling as I do this well?

External Behaviours
Question: What am I doing on the outside?

Ability: To find laughter in life
Question: What exactly am I able to do?

Context
Conversational laughter

(Adapted from Gordon and Dawes 1997, Dilts 1993, Funes 1994)

With this process you can gain awareness of what lies behind your ability to laugh when it works. I have included a blank form for you to record your findings in Appendix 4. You now have a tool to elicit your own theory of laughter and be able to use it whenever you choose to help yourself laugh. I have included below a worked out example of the theory from someone I interviewed for the book. I offer it to you as an example of the kind of information that eliciting your own theory of laughter can give you, and as a model of a theory that has all the components of the kind of healing laughter we have been exploring in this chapter.

A LIVING THEORY OF LAUGHTER: 'GRATEFUL PEOPLE LAUGH'

The key values that Martin lives by are: joy, lightness and community. The most fundamental value we explored was joy. The key beliefs that enable him to experience joy are as follows:

☺ It is possible for everybody to experience joy.

☺ My pain, loneliness and sense of isolation has developed my ability to laugh.

☺ I am amused by people.

☺ I am a curious person.

☺ Every situation has both positive and negatives.

☺ I always believe it is possible to say of things 'it's just not that serious'.

☺ I enjoy the challenge of showing others that there is just not much to be miserable about.

☺ I am lucky and grateful to be alive today. Just look around you!

☺ Life should be about the pursuit of joy.

Martin makes an equivalence between laughter and joy. Hearing the laughter of his children and those he loves is what he means by joy and having a part in helping others get to 'see a glimpse of our smallness in the universe' is for him a reason to live.

Joy is important because it keeps him grounded in the reality of life, because it keeps him alive in spite of the pains of life and because it shows to him daily that 'Okay. I'm right. It's just not that serious!' So it is about the confirmation of a belief that is fundamental to his self-image: that it is always possible for all of us to experience joy, regardless of circumstance.

The diagram below shows in summary form the different aspects of Martin's Living theory of laughter. A key point to highlight about his strategy to find laughter in life is that the Action he is always taking is to pay attention, noticing what is going on around him. The ability to notice enables him to find ways to compare any minor or major event with a contrasting event that helps him connect with the belief that 'it's just not that serious'. What this enables him to do is to have a 'secret survival strategy' to deal with life.

Martin has an ability to notice detail, to look beyond the initial judgement of D-mode and connect with G-mode. As he does this he can then go back to D-mode with more information to help himself find something else *in* the situation to compare with. This has the effect of re-focusing his attention away from the small detail and towards the larger map of life. In relation to being run over by a car, having problems in the bank is just not that serious. Or, in relation to not having any money at all, complaining about the weight of one's shopping bags is just not that serious. Laughter comes from the incongruity that 'I am moaning and cursing about something that, in the larger map of life, has no meaning.' All that has meaning is the experience of joy and gratefulness for being alive.

Martin believes that anything that moves us away from joy should be dealt with in this way. It is just not worth spending one's energy in developing a perspective that stops us from noticing the detail of life. Martin is an example of someone who lives the quote I

MARTIN'S LIVING THEORY OF LAUGHTER

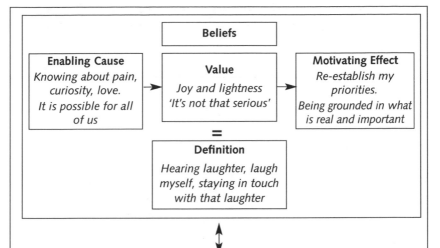

Beliefs

Enabling Cause	**Value**	**Motivating Effect**
Knowing about pain, curiosity, love. *It is possible for all of us*	*Joy and lightness* *'It's not that serious'*	*Re-establish my priorities.* *Being grounded in what is real and important*

=

Definition

Hearing laughter, laugh myself, staying in touch with that laughter

Strategy

I know it's working because of what I don't feel. Feel free from body. If I laugh I don't feel pain.

Primary Operation

Tell myself it's just not worth spending the energy on this.

Secondary Operation

Moan and feel angst for a short time and then go to primary. If I felt it was impossible to achieve I'd turn to drugs! Or die, it's that fundamental.

Emotions

Joy and absence of pain

Actions

Smiling, laughing and pointing out to people what is 'half-full' about their experience. Helping them turn around the meaning of their experience. Paying attention to detail. Noticing what is there.

Ability: To see something humorous in most things. To be able to say of everything 'It's just not that serious!'

offered you at the beginning of this book. It is only when we do not know how to perceive that we do not notice that the whole of life has both pain and joy and that we can choose what we pay attention to.

As we feel pain, we can choose to play with that pain through finding some incongruous comparison to make, to allow us to access our inner laughter place. This may connect us with joy through releasing our pain about the situation, or merely connect us with joy. What the laughter does can be argued from different theoretical perspectives. We can leave the arguments to the experts and still know that laughter helps us survive, still know that what is real is that, as Martin said to me, 'If I can help a child to giggle he does not feel his toothache.'

It is worth noting as we end this section that Martin has scored over 300 in the Holmes and Rahe Social Readjustment Scale. This scale measures key life events and the impact that they have on your susceptibility to stress. So many stressful events have happened in his life that he has had plenty of opportunity to test his theory. He believes that it is partly because of this that he has the ability to find laughter. If he had not developed it, he would not be alive today. He says: 'Everything is funny. I believe that. But I don't want to test this belief any further. I don't want to find out how losing both my legs could be not that serious!' Notice that the sentence presupposes that there would be a way in which losing both his legs could be not serious. This is key to his ability.

> The point was made long ago in the parable of the cup of soup. One man having sipped a while began to moan, 'The cup is already half empty', while his companion, having drunk as much, rejoices, 'It is still half full'.[10]

This section was going to be about Martin's illness and his life, to give you a sense of just how serious all that he has to deal with is. That was my own bias and prejudice. The whole point about his theory of laughter, however, is that no event in life is that serious.

I would have misled you had I chosen to speak about what is 'half-empty' in Martin's life, when his whole identity is about what is 'half-full' in it. To give you a flavour of the other side suffice it to say that, as you read this, he may no longer be alive. And yet, is it not also true of any of us that we may only have a few minutes left? As we ended the interview he said: 'I would sum it all up with one chapter title: "Grateful people laugh". Maybe it should be your last chapter.'

Here are the key tips to remember about Martin's approach:

☺ Pay attention to detail.

☺ Ask yourself, What else is there *in this situation* that can help me confirm that 'it's just not that serious'? (irrespective of how serious I feel it now is)

☺ Filter life through: 'I feel grateful for *everything* in my life. Everything that happens I need.'

The essence of this chapter has been to teach you that if you are going to be laughter independent you had better develop a sense of what laughter means to you in your life. As you understand that you can make choices about when and where you laugh, you gain a stronger sense of self, without the use of expensive therapists! We have looked at how playing with pain can help your emotional development, and we have given you a tool to elicit your own theory of laughter in situations where it works for you.

As you started to explore your laughter theory, you may have come across certain beliefs that don't help you laugh – beliefs that actually limit your ability to laugh, that you may have discovered and want to change. I asked you to record these in a separate piece of paper. Now it is time to attend to those beliefs. The next chapter explores the many ways our beliefs act as barriers to finding our natural laughing place, and you will learn many techniques to help you discover new beliefs that may help you laugh even more every day.

CHAPTER 4

WAYS TO THE INNER LAUGHING PLACE:
CHOOSING OUR BELIEFS

There are many ways in which our beliefs about life and laughter can help us deal with our circumstances. Beliefs are always a resource, even the ones that no longer serve us. We must, therefore, treat our beliefs and those of others with the utmost respect. This is why I talk about updating beliefs rather than changing them. Leave the belief alone and create for yourself a new set of experiences that can help you reorganise the belief. Be clear that beliefs are our logic of the world. Our belief system is the way we make sense of life. We set out to prove what we believe in what we perceive, as we discussed in chapter 1 in relation to the D-mode way of thinking.

We do not set out to test the validity of our beliefs in everything we do. This is useful because it allows us to function without having to validate everything from first principles. If we did not have this resource, simple things would take so long that our daily lives would be unmanageable. Sometimes this logic of the world needs to be updated by new data from the present. We may have some beliefs which are already a resource, but which could become an even more effective resource if they were updated in some way.

Some of our beliefs can create a barrier to healing laughter whilst still helping us preserve order in our world. These beliefs are only limiting in relation to the desired outcome of finding laughter. I want you to keep this in mind as we explore new ways of organising your experience in what follows. I would not want you to gain the impression that your logic of life is wrong. All it needs is more data to do what it does best: generalise and create new order to help you function even more effectively.

That said, you might recognise some of the laughter barriers that follow, not in yourself of course, but in the person sitting next to you!

THE LAUGHTER BARRIERS

Conversation has certain rituals, as we suggested in chapter 2. These rituals can turn into specific games that we play in relation to a particular realm of experience. Laughter is no exception. We have interesting conversational games that we play in relation to laughter. When played according to the rules, these games lead you to create barriers to laughter in your life.

Recognise the game and play by new rules: your own. You can, of course, choose to play by the usual rules and know that this will mean less laughter in your life. This may be what you want in certain situations.

I call these games the laughter barriers. We will explore how we play them in the next few pages. I will also give you some ideas about how else each game could be played if you wanted to use it to break down a barrier rather than create one. I have named each game with the opening line of the conversation. You will recognise each as a common expression in social interaction. I break down what goes on below the explicit social level and within the psychological level. We will learn how common expressions carry within them clear beliefs about the way life 'should' be. Beliefs are, after all, no more than rules for life which we often apply to everyone we know and not just to ourselves.

'WHY ARE YOU LAUGHING? IT'S NOT THAT FUNNY'

You will hear this whenever you are having a good hearty laugh and somebody feels left out or embarrassed by your laughter. People live under the illusion that D-mode is king; that our rational and analytical mode of thinking can take care of everything; that if we do something there must be a reason, and that if there is a reason we must be able to stop whatever we are doing at any time and deliver the precise reason for our action.

If only! Real people work very differently. We act before we know it. We have an altogether different way of thinking that is vital to our ability to function in the world and particularly to our ability to lead creative lives. We will explore creativity in chapter 5. Here it is important for you to know that it is G-mode that is king when it comes to laughter. We often laugh without conscious understanding of the reason. This is not to say that a reason does not exist, but simply that we are not aware of what the reason is.

The impact of the question *Why are you laughing?* is simple: You stop laughing and start to search in D-mode for a reason for the laughter. As we will always construct a story to make any behaviour we engage in plausible, a reason will appear and we will offer a 'because ...' This game does not end here. Once you stopped laughing and offered a plausible reason you then become open to the next move: Is the reason good enough? In other words, will you have offered a good enough reason for the other person to take away the 'not that funny' judgement? You most likely have not. You have lost on both counts. You have played into this laughter barrier and have opened yourself up to be judged as having 'no sense of humour'.

The belief that is at play here is that in order to laugh one must always have a reason available to consciousness and unless there is a reason the speaker cannot join in and must, therefore, judge the situation as not funny. This is the belief that needs to be updated if the end result of the game is to change. You might consider this when designing new responses that may help the speaker reassess the belief: Do not take the judgement or the question at face value. This game has a clear end – to stop your laughter.

So what can you do? A response could be, 'You're absolutely right. It is not funny to you, and my laughter clearly shows you that it's funny to me, whatever the reason.' This will still stop your laughter momentarily, but at least you will be true to yourself and not feel forced to give a reason you do not have. It is important here that you deliver your reply from the spirit of the previous chapter, not with an intention of ridiculing the other but with the intention of playing respectfully with his or her pain.

'THAT'S ENOUGH; LET'S GET BACK TO WORK!'

This game is the one I come across most often in my work in large corporations. A group of people may be working and achieving results, and also may be sharing a lot of laughter and play, a rare sight in any company. There will inevitably be someone in the group who will start this game with the sentence above. Several statements about how nothing had been achieved, how the speaker was right, will follow the 'That's enough. Let's get back to work!'

The impact of this game as it is played out daily in so many offices is twofold. It stops the flow of an integrated way of thinking, G-mode and D-mode working together, and it is used to provide validation for the belief that work results can only be achieved with gravity. Levity is not a state to be associated with important work. If we are laughing we can't be working. So we must stop laughter and start work.

We hold this belief so strongly that I find it almost impossible to get people to realise that they are playing the game. I get asked to come in and do a workshop because 'Employees need to get away from work, and a bit of fun will be good for them before they get back into it'. I point out that I don't do that, but that I will be happy to work with the employees to help them find ways to laugh and work at the same time. Their next sentence is always 'Yes, of course. That's what I meant.' But it wasn't. What they meant was that laughter and work don't mix even if they would very much like them to. Whenever I go into workplaces to hold workshops, I start with an explanation of just how seriously I take my laughter. For my entire working career I have been on the receiving end of this particular game and I have had to deal with the prejudice that comes from this belief.

Let me give you a simple example of how it manifests itself at work. I once asked a colleague at a management institute where I worked to give me feedback to help me assess my performance. It was all very positive generally and as we were chatting about it he said,

'There is only one thing that you may need to watch out for – your laughter and lightness when you are around the place. Whilst I think it's wonderful, some people may think that you are not professional enough. How could I put it? It sometimes is difficult to guess from your approach the depth of knowledge and skill that you have.' In other words, I did not do enough 'serious work'. I may have been working, even when I was laughing, but this is never part of the equation. Laughter gets interpreted as lightweight and lightweight means unskilled. A very tough belief to shift.

I have also found myself on the other side of it many times. I still catch myself thinking, 'Enough laughter. Let's get back to work.' The assumption is that we are not working when we are laughing. Wrong. In order to get results we need ways of thinking and working together and laughter is one way in which we can tell that we are totally present and engaged in activity. There is much more of us working when there is laughter than when there is not. If our emotions have been checked out at the door, how can we be expected to achieve good results?

Taking the risk to be perceived as different can easily change this game. I used to worry about not portraying enough *gravitas* at work. I now explain to all who want to listen about the value of *levitas*, and how the archetype of the fool is also the carrier of wisdom in many cultures; that enlightenment is about *levitas* and not *gravitas*. You still have to hold enough gravitas for those who do not share your belief to listen, though. Redesigning this game is easy. You say to those who start the conversation, 'I don't need to get back to work. Working is exactly what I'm doing as I laugh.' You may also choose to point out how much more effective we can be when we use *all* our cognitive and emotional capabilities in the service of a goal.

'I LOVE HIM BECAUSE HE MAKES ME LAUGH'

This game is one of my favourites. How many times have you heard this one? It is often quoted as the reason certain women choose to enter into a relationship, and I do not believe this is coincidence. Women have until very recently been socialised to be the more passive members of our society and this trait has been slow to change. And passivity is at the core of this game.

The belief at play here is that other people 'make me' laugh or cry; that the responsibility lies with them and not with me and that I will have a relationship with a person who is able to 'make me' laugh. This game results in the validation of a belief that tells me that I am not laughter independent and that I need others in order to laugh. Whilst it is true that a great deal of laughter is social and shared with others, it is important to distinguish this from the dependency assumed by this game.

When I asked Martin about the locus for his laughter, he clearly said that his laughter was self-referenced: 'I laugh a lot on my own, just reflecting on the paradoxes and inconsistencies of human beings. Laugher is all around you. You just need to look.' This is a very different approach from that which this game requires.

Many relationships are based on the creation of dependency loops, where one party takes all the responsibility for particular behaviours. With the responsibility comes also the blame when things are not the way the other party wants them, as in the following poem by Portia Nelson:[1]

> You want to please me ... and,
> I want to please you ...
> So please make a decision
> About where we are going tonight.
>
> If I make a decision and you don't like it
> You'll be mad at me
> And I'll be miserable all evening
> because I haven't pleased you
>
> Now ...if you try to please me ...
> And you make the decision,
> If I don't like it

When we get there ...
At least you will be pleased

If I am unhappy with where we are,
Or what we are doing,
That's all right ...

Because it won't be my decision
That will have made me unhappy.
It will be yours.
Therefore,
It will be your fault!
And that will please me.

We go to such lengths not to take responsibility for our actions! It's so much easier to have someone else to blame when I can't find laughter in my daily life anymore. I guess that is the time when I say, 'He used to make me laugh and that's why I loved him. He doesn't anymore, so I'll leave him.' Still, looking for someone to make me laugh, I can go through life never learning that access to that laughing place can only originate from within; that others can help me laugh, but cannot 'make me' laugh without me sharing at least fifty per cent of the responsibility for that communication.

The way to play this game differently is simply to ask oneself: If he or she wasn't here how would I find laughter in my life? Or what do I need to be doing in my life, independent of this person, to access my inner laughing place? In other words, just looking for people to make me laugh will have me playing a game that keeps me laughter dependent. Independence comes when the locus of control shifts back to me. And yes, the responsibility also!

'HOW CAN YOU LAUGH AT A MOMENT LIKE THIS!?'

A wake is defined as 'a watch over the dead, often involving festivities'. As I talked to Irish people about their experience of a wake, or the waking process as they referred to it, I found a perfect example of what I want you to take away from this little book. The traditional wake requires no invitation. You know the person who has died and you have a duty to attend. Traditionally, an Irish wake lasted a number of days and would have a storyteller in attendance. Many stories would be told about the dead person and a group of women were the 'criers' of the wake. Those attending would come and sit by the criers and 'bawl their eyes out, and then get up and go and have a few cracks'. The laughter came naturally. There were no formal 'laughers'. The laughter would come from the stories that were told in celebration of the dead person's life.

In one ritual is contained a clear counter example of the belief that it is not appropriate to laugh at certain times; particularly when death is close to us. Yet this is only said by those who have not experienced death and suffering at close hand. As we saw in the previous chapter those who are dying or who work with the terminally or critically ill, simply know that laughter heals. Martin's secret survival technique seems to come to the fore when there is also a significant amount of pain in a given situation.

> I think I was in pain. Most of it [laughter] comes from pain. The only defence against that was to laugh at it [the terrible home situation], to find what was funny in it. I had lots of those sights in my youth to frighten me, but also to make me laugh and learn to see what was funny.

This quote does not come from Martin, though it easily could. It comes from Nathan, a highly successful writer and director. A humorist. We will return to him in the next chapter when we explore the creative experience. Here I use his quote as yet another example from somebody who makes it okay for himself 'to laugh at moments like this'.

This game denies the players the most fundamental release valve of all – the possibility to find laughter in pain. And sometimes, as we have said before, there is nothing left for us to do but laugh. The judgement is often made by somebody who holds the belief that to express emotion in public is not appropriate behaviour, but most importantly that laughter does not belong in death. That is how this game gets started. The impact of its first move is to force the laughing person to stop and to start apologising for not maintaining *gravitas* at a moment like this. You need to understand that 'moments like this' are highly culturally determined, as my example of the Irish Wake shows. It would be entirely inappropriate not to laugh at a moment like this if I was waking my mother, for example, in Ireland.

A secondary impact that this game has is that it makes the people who are able to laugh feel ashamed of the emotions they are experiencing. They must learn to not see what is funny in pain. If it helps us survive situations that otherwise may kill us with pain and fear, why would we choose to block out and not see something that is clear and available to all of us?

The way to redesign this game is simple. Go back to the notion of playing with pain respectfully. The only moment that laughter is not appropriate is when this is not respected. If you are playing with your pain respectfully and you have permission to play with other people's pain then when someone starts this particular game you can change it with a simple, 'Would you really like to learn how to laugh at moments such as this?'

The extent to which you care for the other player will determine how much of the new rules you want to share with them!

Now Playing at Kieran's Irish Pub![2]

FLANAGAN'S WAKE

Flanagan's Wake is the hilarious audience-interactive Irish wake that has been playing to sold out houses in Chicago for the past four years under the production of the Zeitgeist Theatre Company. The show is part scripted and part improvised and full of 'Irish Brogue and Blarney!' The comedy takes place in the beautiful fictional town of

Grapplin, County Sligo, Ireland and features an eclectic cast of characters. From the moment the audience arrives until they leave, they are at an 'Irish Wake'. The cast of characters greet audience members as family and long-lost friends. All help recall pertinent details of Flanagan's life (including the way he died – which is improvised differently every show based upon suggestions gathered from the audience) and honour his memory by sharing stories and singing songs about the man himself. Audience members might even find themselves making a claim for the Flanagan land! All of the fun (and mourning) takes place at the fictional wake chapel at Kieran's Irish Pub in downtown Minneapolis, 330 – 2nd Avenue South.

Flanagan's Wake is written and produced by Zeitgeist Theatre in Chicago and has been produced in Chicago, Cleveland, Philadelphia and Rochester, New York. The Minneapolis production was originally directed by two of its Chicago authors, Jack Bronis and Phil Lusardi, with current direction by Phil Lusardi. The inaugural Minneapolis cast included: Ahna Brandvik (BNW alumna), Chris Carlson, Bob Field (BNW Monday Company), Jeff Hopkins, Richard Logan (BNW alumnus), Caleb McEwen (BNW alumnus), Sara Valentine, and Craig Hansen (BNW alumnus) on keyboard.

All performances at Kieran's Irish Pub, 330 – 2nd Avenue South, Downtown Minneapolis.

TICKETS Call the Brave New Workshop at 332-6620 for reservations. Tickets $18 in advance, $20 at the door. Dinner reservations at Kieran's prior to or following the wake must be made separately by calling Kieran's directly at (612) 339-4499.

'THEY LAUGHED A LOT, BUT I DON'T KNOW IF THEY LEARNED'

I catch myself daily playing this particular game. It starts by creating an environment around me that helps people feel free to laugh together. It may be a laughter workshop or a very serious programme on global leadership skills, but my hallmark is always the same – an environment where people can relax and laugh and learn.

I know this to be important for people to learn any content. And yet … I often catch myself wondering if people are having too good a time, and as I reflect on the experience later I wonder if they actually learned anything. The belief that is at play here is that learning and laughter do not mix, that if we are laughing we can't be learning and vice versa. This is so ingrained in us that we even judge the amount of learning by how hard it was to pick up. In playing this game, as we review our experience we reinforce for others and ourselves the clear message that laughter and learning do not mix.

But let's look at the evidence. When we explored the details of learning effectively in chapter 1, we said that emotions are key and that a playful and goalless mode of thinking had to be integrated with a purposeful and analytic way of thinking. We labelled these two thinking modes D-mode and G-mode. One is deliberate. The other creates a gap for solutions to emerge.

Eric Jensen[3] notes a very interesting fact about our brain design. The pathways coming from the midbrain to the neo-cortex are over twice as many as those coming from the neo-cortex to the midbrain. The midbrain is a key site for processing emotions, G-mode thinking. The neo-cortex is a key site for rational thinking, D-mode. We are designed to give priority to our emotions and this makes evolutionary sense. If we are in fear for our life, this should be more important than daydreaming about the solution to that crossword puzzle.

We can know about something in D-mode, and yet not know that we know it until we feel it in our body. The emotional content of experience is needed by us to attach meaning to it. Jensen says that we literally use the saying 'I feel, therefore I am' to process meaning. I do not go as far as he does in my analysis. I believe that both emotion and D-mode thinking are needed for us to learn new things in the world.

If our emotions are engaged, and laughter can be evidence of this, we will remember the experience as having meaning. More of our brain and our body is active and this means that 'if they laughed a lot, they learned'. Laughter activates our neuropeptides, which integrate the communication between our different systems. If our body-mind system is working in an integrated fashion, we will learn more than if only half, or a quarter of it, is activated. This is stating the obvious. Yet years of research have been needed for the development of approaches to learning that embody the idea of attending to emotions and the body. It is sad to note that whilst these approaches are taking hold in the realm of adult learning, they remain a rare sight in the teaching of children.

I work on a daily basis with the products of this old-fashioned kind of education. People arrive at my workshops expecting to be 'told', to be empty vessels into which knowledge will be poured. They are not ready to take any responsibility for their learning. If learning is to happen, they assume, then the experience has to be painful. Learning is therefore something to be avoided.

I understand my role as a teacher to be that of educating people on how we learn, irrespective of what the topic may be; to teach them that learning and laughter can, and should, go together if their learning it to stick. If people are to be motivated to learn for the rest of their lives, rather than run away in fear from any experience that may teach them new ways of living, they must learn to involve their emotions in a positive way.

Once the emotional state is right, the learning of any content becomes easy. But content and teaching skill have to be part of the picture also if learning is to happen. The problem is that all too often we focus only on content and forget that for the content to be relevant it has to be relevant to someone. Putting learning and laughter together in our mind can help us develop a fundamental life skill, an attitude of lifelong learning. We need this if we are going to be able to keep up with the speed of change in our world today.

On a good day, I play the healthy version of this game with myself. I encourage you to do the same. I say 'They laughed a lot. How much did they learn about having a love for learning?' or, when applied to myself, 'Each day I connect laugher with learning I reinforce a life attitude that change is something to thrive on and not avoid.'

What you must not do is fall into the trap of playing the 'mine-is-more-important-than-yours' game. All the components we have discussed are needed for learning. Laughter is important to create the right learning state. Content is important to achieve the result. The priority of each changes at different stages of our learning cycle, but all are needed.

'I CAN'T HELP IT. IT'S JUST THE WAY I AM'

You were not born thinking that, were you? What a lovely question. It changes the perspective of the statement to 'the way I am has changed as I have grown up'. Talk about re-organising experience!

But let's explain the game before we give away the technique of changing its rules. Those people who hold a deterministic model of the world play this game. They include their behaviour and who they are into the overall category of 'What will be, will be' and 'There ain't nothing you can do about it,' if I can be allowed to mix my song lyrics rather than my metaphors.

These people would answer the challenge of the question above thus, 'That is true, but I have had nothing to do with what I have become.' Their actions are their actions. Whatever they do they just can't help it. You hear them say, 'Oh! I know that I should be able to not do this, but I just can't help it.'

You can keep playing this game *ad infinitum*. It's a barrier for laughter. It reinforces the belief that 'life just happens to me and I have no control over it.'

I cannot control the winds, but I can direct the sails. If people who are dying and in concentration camps can find a way to change their perspective to make impossible conditions bearable, then it is possible for us folk to do it too. After all, what are some of the things we say we can't change? Here is a selection:

☺ I can't stop eating chocolate.

☺ I can't help but shout when I don't get my own way.

☺ I can't help but wish that it happened to somebody else.

☺ Life is depressing. I just can't help but see it that way. I just don't know if I want to go on driving this car, and I can't afford a new one.

☺ I just can't trust anybody. I can't help it. I wish I could but I can't. It is just the way I am.

When we say *can't* we mean that we are not prepared to accept the consequences of changing how we view the world and ourselves. If all my interactions with those around me are based on the belief that I have no control, then what would I talk about if my focus shifted? I can shift my focus. Everybody can. When I'm attached to staying the same and I do not want to put in the effort that it would take to change, it is easier to say I can't and not be responsible than to say I choose not to and stay responsible.

If I can say I choose not to, then I can laugh. I can view my behaviour from outside the game and notice myself playing the game. I can say, I am choosing to stay the same and let me learn how this particular way of behaving is helping me. This can open up the door to greater awareness and to the possibility of change. It will certainly lead to a sense of shared responsibility with life for what happens to me in it. It may even lead me to a place where I can make light of my very highly developed ability to hold life responsible for my misfortunes. It is a very useful ability to have. If somebody else is responsible then my sense of self-worth can never change. Whatever happens, it's 'not me'. What may not be so obvious is that if it is 'not me' for those traits I dislike then it is also 'not me' for those traits I like. Self-worth cannot develop under these circumstances.

For as long as I continue to hold to the belief that I can't help it, I feed my sense of being a victim to life. The question is not whether this is true in any absolute sense. That is irrelevant. The question is, Which belief is more likely to keep me alive and trying out new strategies to deal with life's difficulties? The way out of this game is to say to yourself, 'But if I could change it, how will I change it?' or, as a very dear colleague of mine says when she is on the receiving end of this particular game, 'Your story moves me deeply. What is your plan?'

Nobody denies that we all have our past wounds. This is not intended to devalue people's pain. How much time needs to go by, though, before I stop using my past as an excuse for not changing my present or my future? If we want to be healthy, we must stop doing what Caroline Myss calls 'defining ourselves by our wounds'. The many support groups that exist around different wounds (e.g. alcohol, drugs, eating, abuse, and anything that is labelled an addiction) are evidence of our culture's need to define people by their wounds. We will find many tears in this approach, but not much laughter.

When we look at creativity in the next chapter, we will see that extreme life pain seems to be a common characteristic in humorists. It is possible to learn to play with our pain to help us change our world-view; to use laughter as a tool for changing the way I am. I can become aware of inconsistencies in my behaviour, and play with these as a way of learning about myself. This is what I have started to show you in the previous chapters. The pain is always real. The lifetime suffering is optional. But taking responsibility is so scary for us sometimes, that we rather hang on to our suffering for life than be held responsible. What follows are some guidelines for those who want to learn how to choose the way they are.

Once upon a time there was a very old man. The worst rains he had ever seen hit the little town where he lived. The town was flooding. A truck came by to take the old man out of his house to safety. He refused to go. 'No, I won't go with you,' he said. 'The Lord will save me.'

The water levels started to go up. He had to stay on the first floor of his house to avoid drowning. A boat was sent to rescue him. 'No, I won't go with you,' he said. 'The Lord will save me.'

The water levels continued to rise until he found himself on the roof of his house to stay alive. A helicopter arrived to rescue him and he refused to go. 'No, I won't go with you,' he said. 'The Lord will save me.'

The water covered his house and he drowned.

'But Lord,' he said, 'how could you let me die? I trusted that you would save me and you let me die. How could this happen?'

'I sent you a truck, I sent you a boat, I sent you a helicopter …' the Lord said. 'Exactly what else did you want me to do?'

WE CAN CHOOSE 'THE WAY WE ARE'

The last game I presented highlights the fact that we sometimes assume that the beliefs that make up 'who I am' come to us as if by magic and that we cannot change them. Further we assume that if we do change them we will no longer be 'who I am'. The first assumption is not supported by reality; the magic is simply the process of generalising from our experience. The second assumption is right on target. 'Who I am' changes moment by moment and if I choose not to accept this I will spend a great deal of emotional Scrunchies trying to maintain an illusion of consistency and stability over time.

We need to know that we can do an 'inside job' on our model of the world to allow us to respond to outside circumstances in more sustainable ways. Our generalisations belong to us and we can make choices about 'who I am'. If I cannot choose this, who can? If I assume that I cannot, what is the result? I have given over control of who I am to my external environment. Whilst I have no control over what happens in my life, I can choose what I generalise from my experience. And one choice that is available to me is to laugh.

Now we set about learning how to become more flexible in choosing. In a way you already know the essence of this process. Remember the frame shifting activity in chapter 3? I hope it showed you the power of putting different filters on reality. We attach specific meaning to what happens to us and can easily be flexible about looking at the world from different perspectives – so long as we have nothing invested in keeping hold of a given perspective of reality as being The Truth. The problem comes because the way we think is such that we have a lot invested in confirming our beliefs of reality. We sample the world for confirmation and we do this to help us manage our cognitive load.

When we want to keep one particular filter as the only filter, it is often because we want to protect ourselves from the consequences of changing that filter. If I want to be professional, and professional for me means that I don't laugh, then I will find it very hard to laugh at work. It's not that I cannot. It's that I do not want the consequence of being perceived as unprofessional! Even those beliefs that we don't like serve a purpose in some context. It's all about frames and reframes. Let me explain.

Framing is the process we use to select, delete and arrange our thoughts. It's the way we make meaning. A frame is a mental pattern or map that enables us to make sense of a given set of experiences. If we share the same frame of reference, we will put the same meaning on a given event. This will lead us both to behave in similar ways. Without framing we cannot think. We can just perceive what is at a given moment. Framing allows us to generalise from our detailed day-to-day perception. Beliefs are examples of particular frames we put around events. The frame will direct our perception of the data that we notice in D-mode thinking, from all that is available in G-mode.

To explain reframing[4] I want to tell you an ancient story:

> Once upon a time there was a very old farmer in a very small village. He was very wealthy because he had a horse that he could use for his farming work. One day the horse ran away.
>
> 'Very bad luck,' said the neighbours.
>
> 'Maybe,' said the farmer.
>
> A few days later the horse came back with two new friends – two wild horses he had met on his journey.
>
> 'What good luck,' said the neighbours.
>
> 'Maybe,' said the farmer.
>
> The next day one of his sons tried to ride one of the new horses. He broke his leg.
>
> 'Very bad luck,' said the neighbours.
>
> 'Maybe,' said the farmer.
>
> The next week the army came to the village to take young men to fight in the war. They did not take the farmer's son because of his broken leg.
>
> 'What good luck,' said the neighbours.
>
> 'Maybe,' said the farmer.

The meaning of the same event is judged positive or negative in the light of what we compare our event with. Reframing is the process whereby we change the frame of an event and through that change we change the meaning the event has. Any event in life can have more than one meaning. We can find laughter or tears, depending on the frame we choose to put around what happens to us.

We can change the meaning of an event or we can change the context of where that event occurs.

Meaning reframe

If the limiting belief that you want to reframe has the form 'I feel x when y happens' it is generally useful to do a meaning reframe on it. Y stays constant and what changes is x.

Ask yourself some of the following questions:

☺ What is a larger or different frame that could provide a new meaning to x in which x could have a positive value?

☺ What other aspect of this situation could change its meaning?

☺ What else could this behaviour mean?

☺ How else could y be described?

What you want here is to find a frame, like in the farmer story, where what the behaviour means is useful and positive for you or the person you are talking to. If somebody has been looking at something from a half-empty point of view, you will often get laughter as you change the meaning to something that he or she had not considered.

Example:

'I feel angry when I see dirty footprints in the carpet.'

'Imagine there being no footprints, and know that this means you are alone ... And now I want you to notice those footprints and know that this means that those people you care about are nearby.'

The context reframe

When the limiting belief has the form of 'I'm too x' you usually want to do a context reframe. You search for a context where x would be appropriate.

You can ask yourself the following questions:

☺ In what context would x have value?

☺ How many different contexts can I think about?

☺ Which one can help me change my evaluation of x?

Example:

'I'm too stubborn.'

'And I want you to know that that stubbornness can allow you stand up for yourself – when others try to impose their views on you.'

Are you starting to get the hang of this? Reframing is at the basis of many jokes, of many approaches to therapy and of many a political speech. We can use language to change the way we think and we do this without purpose and without knowing. The rest of this chapter will give you the tools to change the way you think through the words you use with purpose and knowledge.

The category game[5]

The purpose of this activity is to practise the fine-grained behaviour of creating new categories to organise our experience. We are fleshing out the answer to the question, How do we turn everything that happens to us into the kind of experience that can bring us laughter? Categories are our labels for what we experience and are also frames of reference that have a greater level of generality than the data they describe.

☺ This game requires five players. Get your friends playing it next time you get together!

☺ Each person chooses a word as follows:

- Name something.

- Next person names something else that is totally different.

- Next person names something else that is different again.

☺ Once you have 5 words, direct your attention to the following question:

- What possible overall category could I put those into? Each person to generate a category individually. Warning: The object of the game is not to say, 'No, it isn't.' Everyone is entitled to his or her category.

☺ Get each person to share and explain the rationale for his or her category to the others around the following questions:

- What did you do to create your category?

- How did you get to it?

- How did you organise your experience to generate the category?

You may discover that a category is no more than a set of relationships that are made explicit in the naming of the category. You may also discover that human beings can make sense of everything! As an extra fun step you may choose to play a story-telling game in which you each have to take turns telling a story, using all the words and the categories that you have generated.

The redefinition game[6]

This game helps you learn another aspect of reframing. We make one-way connections between particular behaviours and their significance, e.g. when I believe that 'I am boring' and make up a category 'boring' that contains many examples of data where I was boring. The category fits in a bigger frame of what I know about myself, my know-how. This know-how in turn fits into the even larger frame of 'What is the purpose of using my know-how?'

This game gets you to ask a number of questions to help you add new data to your belief and also understand more how having the information that 'I am boring' fits in the overall system of who you are. In other words, it can help you redefine the value of that which you now evaluate as negative. This may encourage you to make new connections to your inner laughing place. Here are the steps:

☺ Label: How is 'I am boring' a problem to you?

It is a problem because it stops me from finding laughter in my life. It means that I can't laugh.

☺ Behaviour: What is the behaviour?

Boredom

☺ Elements of the behaviour: How do you do it?

I speak in a monotone voice, an even tempo.

☺ New contexts: Where, when, would you also speak with a monotone voice?

- When I want others to understand me.

- When I speak to a foreign national.

- If I'm on holidays.

- If I'm reading a report for spelling mistakes.

- When I want to send myself to sleep.

☺ Purpose: What purpose can the monotone voice serve?

It can help me be clear and understood by others.

☺ Outcome: In order to do what?

Get what I want

☺ Template for new definition of belief:

> *So this [behaviour] is merely an [element] which is/has [purpose], which you have in order to achieve [outcome].*
>
> *'So this boredom is merely a voice quality which helps you be clear, and which you have in order to get what you want.'*

What this technique achieves is to move the statement away from the level of identity. It is no longer 'I am boring' but 'I have a behaviour called boredom.' The behaviour then gets redefined in a new way that may allow you make new connections about what was a problem. A problem can also be a resource – in this case a resource for clarity. So the behaviour of boredom can mean I don't laugh. It can also mean I can be understood clearly if I speak with an even tempo, what I call a monotone voice. When I notice this, I laugh! I can't be boring then.

What this game does is to get you into the habit of understanding that a generalisation we make about the world is only one of many possible generalisations. We can choose to re-organise our experience and make a new connection. This game helps you learn the power of possibility. Martin, in the last chapter, said that it is the knowledge that laughter is possible that gives his survival technique its power and not that he can always find laughter in what happens to him. The most important skill in the art of living is our ability to create for ourselves the direction of 'yeah, it is possible.' This game helps you do just that.

We have explored some of the most common barriers to finding laughter in life and you may have recognised yourself in one or more of them. I have related how, just as you could play the 'frame shifting' game in the previous chapter, you could learn the technique of reframing meaning and content of life events to help you find new perspectives. The last question that we need to answer in this chapter is: 'And just how else can I use conversation to reorganise my beliefs?'

THE LANGUAGE OF LAUGHTER

As you learned about the laughter questions to give you a strategy for playing with pain, you can also learn about the laughter patterns to give you a way to reframe your own limiting beliefs and those of other people when you want to encourage laughter around you.

Select a key belief that limits your laughter quotient and write it at the top of a blank page. You are about to put it through the laughter patterns! After you have completed this exercise you may find yourself having at least 5 different ways in which you could choose to update your belief. The purpose of this is to help you 'get a glimpse of your smallness in the universe' by noticing that a focus on what limits you is only one of the many ways in which you could choose to organise your experience. I will choose one belief too and use it as an example to help you learn the Laughter Patterns.[7]

Beliefs, limiting or useful, have a clear linguistic structure and there are some simple questions you can ask to help yourself and others update them. The table below introduces you to the general structure of beliefs. Note that beliefs will always have one of those forms; learn to spot them in your conversations.

Belief Structure	What to do
Simple Conjunction: A simple 'and' connecting two otherwise unrelated experiences: 'and ... and'	See Cause-Effect
Implied Causative: A causal connection between two experiences: *before, after, following, as, when, during, while*	See Cause-Effect
Cause-Effect: A statement that states a direct relationship between two experiences: *a causes b*	'Laughing causes me confusion.' Q: 'How specifically does it cause you confusion?'
Mind-Reading: A statement that claims to know someone's internal experience	'He thinks I'm not serious.' Q: 'How do you know he thinks you are not serious?'
Complex Equivalence: When two different experiences are stated as having the same meaning: *a means b*	'Laughter means I'm not capable.' Q: 'How specifically does it mean that?' 'If I laughed would you think I'm not capable?'
Lost Performative: A value judgement that leaves out who performed the judgement and how it was made.	'It's cruel to laugh when someone is ill.' Q: 'Cruel according to whom?' 'If the ill person laughed would that also be cruel?'

So much for the structure of beliefs. It is useful for us to know this when we need to learn to recognise them. Now let's move on to the fun part: the laughter patterns. We will use just two sample structures from the table above, the Cause and effect and the Complex equivalence. A bit of a mouthful? Forget the jargon. Use the examples below to match your own beliefs to the patterns and play. As with grammar, we know the fancy labels exist but we don't need them in order to use it correctly.

THE LAUGHTER PATTERNS

Before we go any further, find a limiting belief you have around laughter that you would not mind updating. Write it down in the following form to help you change it even more easily:

' **x causes y**' My example: 'Laughter causes others to think I'm not capable.'

or

'**x means y**' My example: 'Laughter means I am not learning.'

We will now put these two through the Laughter Patterns and see the impact that this can have on them. Your task is to do the same with your belief and notice how it helps you re-organise your experience. Who knows, you may find that your limiting belief ends up giving you a few unexpected laughs as you play respectfully with it.

I have structured what follows as if it were a conversation between two people, to help you understand the process. One person states the belief and the other uses the Laughter Pattern to reframe his or her experience. The process lends itself equally well to a conversation with yourself! And as I said before, it is always wise to start with yourself.

The words in italics define the cognitive strategy that you are to adopt to generate a new sentence from each pattern. Have fun playing and remember, change is optional!

1. Chunking up – *What is this an example of?*

   Mary: 'Laughter causes others to think I'm not capable.'

   John: 'And everyone also thinks that you are human.'

   Mary: 'Laughter means I am not learning.'

   John: 'And it could also mean that you are learning about the conditions in which you learn.'

2. New world model – *What other model of the world do I know that may change this?*

   Mary: 'Laughter causes others to think I'm not capable.'

   John: 'It may also cause others to think that capability includes your ability to laugh.'

   Mary: 'Laughter means I am not learning.'

   John: 'In my experience it can also mean that I have a new insight.'

3. Find intent – *What is the positive intent behind this belief?*

   Mary: 'Laughter causes others to think I'm not capable.'

   John: 'Does that mean that you want to be capable?'

   Mary: 'Laughter means I am not learning.'

   John: 'And that also means that learning is important to you. How can laughter mean learning?'

4. Stepping up values – *How can I direct attention to a value that is more important?*

   Mary: 'Laughter causes others to think I'm not capable.'

   John: 'Would you rather they thought you were emotionally immature?'

   Mary: 'Laughter means I am not learning.'

John: 'What may be more important is that they know you are alive.'

5. Spell out consequences – *How can I attend to an effect of the belief that may help re-organise it?*

Mary: 'Laughter causes others to think I'm not capable.'

John: 'One consequence of your thinking that is that you increase your stress levels.'

Mary: 'Laughter means I am not learning.'

John: 'And if you keep stopping yourself from laughing you will not be alive to learn.'

6. Chunking down – *How can I make the elements so specific that the stated relationship is re-organised?*

Mary: 'Laughter causes others to think I'm not capable.'

John: 'When you say not capable, what is it that you have found yourself unable to do?'

Mary: 'Laughter means I am not learning.'

John: 'What kind of laughter specifically means that to you?'

7. Self-reference – *How can I use the sentence stated to re-organise the belief it describes?*

Mary: 'Laughter causes others to think I'm not capable.'

John: 'And as you think that, how capable do you feel?'

Mary: 'Laughter means I am not learning.'

John: 'And can you laugh as you learn about that?'

8. Reality check – *What evidence is there to support or disqualify the stated belief?*

Mary: 'Laughter causes others to think I'm not capable.'

John: 'I remember John yesterday saying how capable you were while you laughed at his joke.'

Mary: 'Laughter means I am not learning.'

John: 'Today you did not learn the point of the lecture. Were you laughing?'

9. Redefining sides – *Which element can I replace to change the connotations of the stated belief?*

Mary: 'Laughter causes others to think I'm not capable.'

John: 'Sleeping also causes others to think you are not capable.'

Mary: 'Laughter means I am not learning.'

John: 'Laughter also means you are alive' or 'Pulling your hair out can also mean that you are not learning!'

10. Chunking laterally – *What is an analogy that changes its possible meaning?*

Mary: 'Laughter causes others to think I'm not capable.'

John: 'That's like saying that crying will make others think you are a genius.'

Mary: 'Laughter means I am not learning.'

John: 'That's like saying that sweating means you are cold.'

11. Counter exampling – *I must find a counter example. I just can't help it. Except sometimes.*

Mary: 'Laughter causes others to think I'm not capable.'

John: 'Does not laughing cause them to think that you are capable?'

Mary: 'Laughter means I am not learning.'

John: 'And as children discover new words they laugh.'

12. New desired outcome – *How can I question the relevancy of this belief by setting a new task/activity to help re-organise it?*

Mary: 'Laughter causes others to think I'm not capable.'

John: 'How much have you checked that out with others?'

Mary: 'Laughter means I am not learning.'

John: 'You may want to check what laughter means to others before accepting that belief for yourself.'

What all these patterns are helping you achieve is to explore the frame of reference to which the belief belongs. This can enable you to find new ways of assigning meaning to your experience. A belief is no more than a generalisation about the world, shorthand to allow us to achieve what we want. A limiting belief is a generalisation that needs updating because it is getting in the way of your achieving something you want: to increase your laughter quotient!

These patterns can be summarised as doing 3 things:

☺ They enlarge the frame of reference – thus help you see a bigger picture within the same frame.

☺ They specify particular elements within a frame of reference – thus helping you focus on the specifics that led you to form the belief.

☺ They shift you to a different frame of reference – thus expanding the frames in which you can fit the belief.

They are, in short, simple ways to reframe your beliefs to help you laugh more.

RETURNING TO THE SOURCE: TURNING BELIEFS INTO DATA

We said the laughter patterns are ways to help you specify particular elements within a frame of reference or help you shift to a new frame. Sometimes it is not enough just to get to one belief. We need ways to re-connect with the actual examples of experience that led us to make a given generalisation. Sometimes that is the only way in which we will allow ourselves to re-organise a particular belief; when we can see that the tangible data on which it is based is no longer relevant to who we are today.

We humans have a very simple way of structuring our internal world. We do it the same way as we take the world in, through our senses. If we pay attention to the way we talk we will notice that as well as talk about the football match, we also talk about how we are thinking about it in our heads. The ability to distinguish these two levels of language, structure and content, can be called conversational literacy. We need conversational literacy in order to have the ability to continually give our internal world a spring clean. Otherwise we end up with lots of virtual cobwebs that get in the way of our achieving the results we want.

Remember that laughter happens each time we perceive something anew. The 'spring clean' is therefore a way to get to laughter more often that we do now. Get a friend involved in learning this next set of tools and you will find yourself using smiles and laughs of all grades, from chuckles to explosive laughs, as you talk about your problems and what you believe about them. You will find yourself, easily and smoothly, shifting frames of reference and re-organising your internal world.

Over time this will give you an internal world without cobwebs and a significantly higher laughter quotient. Read on.

MODALITY LANGUAGE

We take information from the external world through the use of five modalities: visual, auditory, kinaesthetic, gustatory, olfactory. Psychologists have argued long and hard over the cognitive reality of mental imagery and will continue to argue in the foreseeable future. Let us assume that the senses are used internally to process and store information and we then have a clear and practical way to begin to make guesses about what is going on 'inside someone else's head'.

Here are some examples of what to attend to in conversation to become literate beyond words and to be able to acquire high quality data from those around you. As you attend to these words you will get clear cues as to how people are organising their internal experience. This will give you ways to help them re-organise their experience to find more laughter in the situations they recount. Again, this can apply to self. As you hear yourself talk, you can notice the way you talk about a problem and get back to the sensory data that helped you form a particular belief about that situation and re-assess it.

Visual	Auditory	Kinaesthetic
Picture, clear, focus, perspective, see, flash, bright, outlook, spectacle, glimpse, preview, short-sighted, distinguish, illustrate, delineate, paint, cloud, clarify, graphic, show, reveal, expose, screen	Tune, note, accent, ring, shout, growl, tone, sound, hear, say, ask, harmonise, key, muffle, rattle	Touch, handle, throw, shock, impact, sharpen, impress, strike, handle, grapple with, getting a handle on, tangible, forward, backward, behind

We refer to this language as modality language, and it is useful to target in conversation if you want to understand how you or somebody else organises their experience. For example, in the statement 'what I see is that laughter at work is unprofessional,' we can target the term 'see'. You can then ask, 'Tell me how you see that.' This helps the person focus on how he or she is thinking about the belief and may act as a guide to a new frame for the belief: 'Well, I see a bunch of employees on the floor playing giggle belly and feel that is no way to behave ... but maybe giggle belly is not part of it?'

SUBMODALITY LANGUAGE

Submodalities are the component elements within a given sensory modality. As I see a picture internally, it has certain characteristics that are independent of the content of the picture. A simple example may serve to show the distinction I am making here. Imagine a picture hanging on a wall. It may be an image of a skiing scene; this is the content. It has, however, certain characteristics: the colours that have been used to paint it, the frame it has around it, the clarity of the image, the location of the picture on the wall, etc.; this is its structure. Submodalities are the parameters that can be investigated and will hold different values for different people. The tables below show some examples.

Visual	Auditory	Kinaesthetic
Colour/black and white, brightness, contrast, focus, texture, detail, size, distance, shape, border, location, movement, orientation, singular image, associated/dissociated, proportion, dimension	Location, pitch, tonality, melody, inflection, volume, tempo, rhythm, duration, mono/stereo	Quality, intensity, location, movement, direction, speed, duration

There is a set of questions that can help us elicit this kind of structure.[8]

Visual	Auditory	Kinaesthetic (tactile and proprioceptive)
– Is the image you see in colour, in black and white, or a mixture of both? – Are the colours vivid or washed out?	– Do you hear the voice as if coming from inside or outside? – Where does the sound originate from? – Is it high pitched or low pitched?	– How would you describe the feeling in your body: Tingling, warm, cold, relaxed, tense? – How strong is the sensation?

Visual	Auditory	Kinaesthetic (tactile and proprioceptive)
– What is the contrast like?	– Is the pitch higher or lower than normal?	– Where is the feeling in your body?
– Is the image sharp in focus, is it fuzzy or blurry?	– What is the tonality: nasal, full and rich, thin, grating?	– Is there movement in the sensation?
– Are there background and foreground details?	– Is it monotone or melodic?	– How long does the sensation last?
– How big is the picture?	– Which parts are stressed?	– What is the texture?
– How far is the image?	– How loud is it?	
– Where is the image located in space? Show me with both hands where you see the image.	– Is it fast or slow?	
	– Does it have a beat or cadence?	
– Is it a movie? Is it still?	– Is it continuous or intermittent?	
– Do you see yourself? Or is it as if you were there?	– Do you hear the sound in one side, both sides, or is it all around you?	
– Do you see the images sequentially or simultaneously?		

Modality and submodality language allows us to explore our experience. It gives us direct access to the structure of our thoughts. And it is here that we can make new choices. It is here that we can find our naturally occurring laughter. The key to learning to listen to this level of language is in paying close attention to the actual words used rather than the meaning they have in the context they are being used. The aim is to listen for the modality words. Once you've got these, it is possible to use submodalities to explore further. For example, if I say, 'I have to build up my picture of him,' you can target 'build up' as an example of a kinaesthetic word. You can then ask me, 'The direction of what you are building is up; at what speed are you building the picture?' You are starting to explore other submodalities to gather more detail about how I am thinking about this picture that I'm building up. Firstly, I would not have expected you to ask that. Secondly, it will get me paying attention to my internal world. A new perception in D-mode is likely to happen and I may well smile at the 'picture' I was building in my head but had not consciously noticed.

META-MODEL PATTERNS

Meta-model patterns[9] are useful when your thinking about a problem is a barrier to you finding a solution to that problem. When all you can see is the half-empty side of life, you need help to find the half-full side. Learn to notice these language patterns and you have yet another way to keep spring-cleaning your internal world and creating ways to get to your inner laughing place. The table below gives you a set of clues to help you expand the frame of reference from which you view a particular problem. As you ask yourself the questions linked to each clue, you can gather more of the specific data that has led you to form that belief about the situation. As you have more connection with the source of your beliefs you can make choices to update them.

Take a problem you are currently experiencing and do some automatic writing. The only rule with this kind of writing is that once you start writing you do not stop. This is to prevent you evaluating what you write. Write down in this free flow manner all your thoughts about this problem. You can then use this text to help you learn the patterns in the table on pp 132–3. I guarantee you that you will not view your problem in the same way afterwards.

Once you have written your text, highlight the patterns you notice and then go through, asking yourself the question associated with the pattern. Notice the many ways in which as you ask yourself the question it shifts your internal experience and helps you view the problem in many different ways. Once again if the jargon for each pattern helps you, use it; if it does not, just compare the example given in the table and the sample words with your text and learn to use the questions. Enjoy the game. But be warned; your problems will never be the same again and the belief 'I just can't change that' will most certainly change!

The questions to use are summarised below. Each pattern in the meta-model is an access point for the modality language that we explored in the last section. You can have access to the origin, the source of the beliefs you hold about a given experience. Go through this process with a problem and try to stay the same; it just can't happen ... but what would happen if it did?

Meta-model questions

- How, what, where, when specifically?

- How do you know that x means y?

- What else could it mean?

- What would happen if you did/didn't?

- Are there any exceptions?

- What stops you?

- How is x significant?

- What does x accomplish for you?

You have access to how you create your model of the world and once you have that you can choose how you structure it. By the way, 'meta' means 'about'. The tool you have just learned is a model about language and hence its name!

On page 134 I offer you activities that can help you integrate your theoretical understanding into your daily behaviour. Laughter will come much more easily when you can gain perspective and understanding about the many creative ways in which we humans structure our problems!

The Meta-Model

Pattern name	Definition	Sample words
Prepositions	The spatial and directional terms	in, out, within, through
Nominalisation	Where an action or process word is referred to as if it were an object, a thing or a person	curiosity, knowledge, relationship, inflation
Unspecified referential index	Noun or object is not specified	it, they, someone, them
Complex equivalence	Two different experiences that are stated as meaning the same thing	a skill cannot be made explicit and that means it is unconscious
Presuppositions	The smallest segments of a sentence that are assumed to be true in order for the sentence to be understood	'I regret that Harry left' 'I don't regret that Harry left' 'Harry left'. Both the first and the second sentence assume the truth of the third.
Modal operators of possibility	Statements identifying what is possible	might, could, may
Universal quantifiers	Broad generalisations	all, never, always
Modal operators of necessity	Statements identifying rules or limits	can't, must, should, shouldn't
Unspecified verbs	Details of action or relationship is not defined	understanding, become aware of, experience, think, sense

Example	Question
The meaning is right there in the words.	When you say 'in' the words, how do you see that?
Inflation is crippling me.	What specifically do you mean by inflation?
You just do that and then you have the solution.	What do you do, specifically?
The test results mean failure.	How specifically do the test results mean failure?
The solution is built up a bit at a time.	How do you know that you are building the solution? What kind of building is the solution?
You could diagnose the fault without the test.	What would happen if you did? What would happen if you didn't?
It is always this result.	Always? Are there no exceptions?
You can't diagnose the fault without the test.	What would happen if you did? What would happen if you didn't? What stops you?
As I think about making a diagnosis.	How specifically do you think about it?

The Meta-model Game

1. Find a few people to have a conversation with and make a decision on a subject you will all talk about. You will need to explain some of the theory you have learned, to make it possible for them to play. Or you may choose to use any conversation and play the game in the comfort of your own mind without any explanation.

2. Your task is to talk about your subject using one of the following categories, a simplified version of the patterns above:

   • Universals: All, every, each, always, forever

   • Imperatives: Must, have to, should

   • Nouns: They, managers, it, company policy, that

   • Verbs: Processing, enjoying, hating, thinking

   • Limitations: Can't, mustn't, shouldn't.

3. Spend a few minutes talking about the same subject using each of the categories above. Stop and check internally how you feel before moving on to the next.

4. What was the effect of using each? How easy was it to do?

This activity will give you an indication of what your preferred language patterns are for structuring what you know. In order to have a body of knowledge about anything we need to generalise, distort and delete sensory data and thus create a consistent model. We simplify when we structure a domain, and we have personal preferences as to the language patterns we use for this process. This activity will have told you about the patterns that are part of your cognitive map, those that you felt comfortable using. And those that are not yet part of your map are those you found tough to use in your conversation.

Asking Meta-model questions

1. For this activity you need to enlist the help of two friends. Assign yourselves a letter each: A, B and C. A talks, B listens and asks questions, C observes. You will all get to be each letter, so don't fight!

2. A chooses a work problem to talk about. B explores that problem using any of the following questions to target the particular type of words; the different meta-model patterns which A uses when talking about her problems.

   - Universals: All, every, each, always, forever.
     Echo universal 'All?' 'Are there any exceptions?

   - Imperatives: Must, have to, should.
     'What would happen if we did/didn't?'

   - Nouns: They, managers, it, company policy, that.
     'Who, what, which specifically?'

   - Verbs: Processing, enjoying, hating, thinking.
     'How specifically?'

   - Limitations: Can't, mustn't, shouldn't.
     'What compels us to do ...?' 'What prevents us from ...?'

3. B's task is to get to the sensory information that exists below each meta-model pattern by only using the questions. You are asking for the other's map of the world, how A thinks about the problem; you are not there to talk about yours. Resist the temptation!

4. A talks about the problem that he/she is experiencing at work. As B asks questions A begins to get more data as to how he/she is thinking about the problem and may find out how else the problem can be perceived, thus finding the laughter in what was the problem.

5. C listens only to modality language and meta-model patterns and writes them down. You are not there to be part of the conversation. Your outcome is to have a list of the words used by the end of your round to share with A and B.

6. Talk for 10 minutes and swap letters so that everyone gets to be each letter.

There is a lot more to learn about the structure of language beyond the immediate content of the words used. The level of conversational literacy you will achieve by practising the activities we have included in this section will be more than sufficient for your laughter quotient development.

We have explored some common limiting beliefs about laughter and you have learned some comprehensive ways to change, re-organise and update the beliefs you choose. The beliefs that make up your model of the world should be those that enhance your health and well being. Having beliefs that give you permission to laugh when you choose, can only enhance your well being. You now have the tools to increase your laughter quotient as much as you dare!

A final word of warning. You will know when it's right for you to play respectfully with beliefs that need updating. Trust yourself to leave them alone for as long as you feel that they are just fine the way they are; even if they don't allow you as much laughter as you would like to have access to. One day you will be ready to reframe them, and then you will know how. Until that day comes, know that everything we do we do for a purpose. Yes, even those things that at D-mode level we can only perceive as useless. This warning also applies to the times you want to use the tools you have learned, to enhance the laughter quotient of others. The best advice is simply not to try. Let them do as they do and focus on you becoming the change you want to see in them.

And if in spite of this warning you are tempted to play, then do it always with permission and never disrespectfully. At worst nothing will change. At best you might get yourself and others to a few new perceptions, which may or may not bring you some laughs.

CHAPTER 5

HA HA! LEADING TO AHA:
LAUGHTER IS CREATIVITY

As we begin to close our exploration of laughter, in this chapter we focus on creativity. We can only be creative in our lives when we have the gift of perspective, but more importantly when we are able to generate many different ways of perceiving the world in a purposeful way. This was the focus of the last chapter. Laughter can lead to new insights and can give us access to our creative self. In this chapter you will find even more tools to enhance your relationship with your creative self. You will understand why it is important to have the courage to 'play the fool' if you are to keep your soul alive through your life, and have the quality of life you deserve.

> I am lost.
> I have gone to find myself.
> If I should return before I get back please ask me to wait.
> Thank you.

WHAT IS CREATIVITY?

A very simple question to get us going. Here is the formula:

$$A+B \leftarrow\rightarrow C!^1$$

You think I'm joking, don't you? The article where this formula appears is a serious article on the links between creativity and humour. The formula is meant to represent a definition of creativity as the linking of two components A and B into a new or original pattern C. Given that sometimes creativity is not just about invention but can be about the discovery of a pattern, we must have a double arrow to indicate that the pattern can also be discovered. And that is that, creativity defined in a precise way.

If only! There are as many definitions of creativity as there are people interested in it. These definitions will highlight particular aspects of the process, depending on the context and the values of the people doing the defining. Without further ado, I want to give you a definition from Thomas Moore that fits with the world-view I am sharing with you in this book: 'Creativity is the process of using our imagination to continue the creation of the world, the process of further elaborating on the world itself.'[2]

Thomas Moore has influenced very significantly my own world-view. His perspective on creativity is closely related to that of Arthur Koestler, which we will be looking at soon. The focus of this view is that we need to look at creativity not as something that is high-flying and the property of a few gifted individuals, but as something that we all have and can use to help us live the ordinary life with soul. Moore uses an example from the composer Stravinsky to explain his own view of creativity; creating music was to Stravinsky 'like making shoes'. The image here is not one of inspiration but one of perspiration – the maker, the fabricator who is dedicated to his or her craft. You do your work and put in your time. In this sense, we can view creativity as the process of 'everyday-making'.

I use everyday-making in the same way as Mary Catherine Bateson talks about 'composing a life'. She suggests that a key skill in the art of living is to understand that we can no longer live under the pretence that we know the end before we set out to live our lives. We must be able to recognise the value in 'lifetimes of continual redefinition'. We must learn to 'discover the shape of our creation along the way' as it is no longer possible to hang on to the illusion of stability. Our lives are complex and the world changing at speeds to which we cannot adapt if adaptation is understood as mapping out a route. By the time we have the route, the landscape has changed again and we can find ourselves in a never-ending process of 'route making'. What we need to do instead is to learn to lead the creative life in the sense we have just defined. Creativity becomes a process of acting in the world to continually put together the familiar in unfamiliar ways and of finding existing pattern rather than imposing pattern. This, according to Bateson, is the skill we need to value and develop if we are going to be able to survive progress. If the process of creativity is a matter of survival, as this view implies, then the development of our creativity is certainly no laughing matter.

In keeping with my assumption that just because something is important it need not be serious, I want to help you make some connections that will allow you to use laughter to develop your ability to live the creative life. Creativity is a gift that we all possess but don't all use, and laughter is a gift that we all posses but don't all use. The similarities don't end there.

Arthur Koestler was one of the first psychologists to connect laughter and creativity and he is responsible for the concept that I have used to title this chapter – the idea that laughter can lead us to the act of creation. He suggests that laughter, the luxury reflex, can be used as evidence that we have put together 'two habitually incompatible associative contexts'. The emotions that are associated with the sudden understanding and putting together of unfamiliar realms of experience are often mixed. We favour laughter when our reasoning process ascertains that no danger is present. The understanding of jokes is an example of the process he describes.

A joke works because you believe that it will take you in a familiar direction, but it suddenly makes a jump to connect the familiar with the unfamiliar. The story does not follow your expectations and as you discover this new connection you laugh. To Koestler this is the essence of the creative act; 'by connecting previously unrelated dimensions of experience, it enables [man] to attain a higher level of mental evolution. It is an act of liberation – the defeat of habit by originality.'

Koestler uses three archetypes to describe human activity: the jester, the sage and the artist. He argues that the underlying mechanism of thought used by us when we engage in humour, or discovery, or art, are the same. The process is, as we have said, the putting together of two habitually incompatible frameworks of experience. As we do this we have choices about what we do with the result of combining both realms. At times we laugh; the jester in us resolves the incongruity between the two realms through a joke perhaps. At times we have an aha-experience; the sage in us makes a discovery that may need to be tested and explored further. And at other times we notice the connections and incongruities but do not change them; the artist in us may write a poem for example.

Koestler believes that curiosity, or the exploratory drive as we referred to it in earlier chapters, is as fundamental a drive in human behaviour as hunger or thirst. He cites extensive evidence from the animal world to show that certain animals, apes for example, will play with a problem and solve it without the offer of a reward. More importantly performance improves when they are not striving for a reward but play with the problem in the spirit of 'l'art pour l'art'. If there is striving there is not true play and the animals 'get impatient and try short-cuts'. This makes the performance decrease. Does this remind you of any animals you know?

When we talked about the many theories of laughter we said that perception, or more specifically the experience of a new perception, was often accompanied by laughter. We can begin to put this insight together with the 'aha-experience' in this chapter. Laughter is the demonstrable behaviour that accompanies our exploratory drive being fulfilled. We can, and do, get stuck in habitual patterns. Koestler suggests that we will attack a problem in habitual ways first. If we know a strategy that has worked for us in the past we will use that first, particularly if 'the same task is encountered under relatively unchanging conditions in a monotonous environment'. He suggests that familiarity will lead us to respond to our environment in stereotypical ways and that 'flexible skills will degenerate into rigid patterns'. Naturally-occurring laughter is a clue to the places in our lives where we are *not* operating from these rigid patterns. We must cultivate this way of being because it is the most fundamental way to grow in our ability to respond flexibly to life's demands.

We are curious animals and can only survive in our world if we have ways of satisfying our curiosity. True play is the way in which human animals do this. Our society does not value true play for adults. We are taught to strive. We therefore become impatient, take shortcuts and then are surprised when our performance drops.

The act of creation is not a matter of luxury; it is a matter of survival. Developing our ability to find laughter in our life will help us get closer to our creativity because laughter is our link with true play. True play is our link to the kind of thinking that allows us to view life as a constant process of redefinition. Laughter can be a sign that we are learning new patterns, that we have grasped a new way of seeing something. In short, laughter can be a measure of how much and how actively we are participating in the process of the creation of every day. The ability to see laughter in the whole of life can lead us to develop the ability of 'composing' our lives. Even in death.

> And give those books to somebody who could use them ... give them to my lawyer. Man on his way to the electric chair, pointing to the legal books he had used to help in his defence.

Creativity is not a way to get out of ordinary life, but of being able to live the ordinary life as an ever unfolding work-in-progress, 'something crafted from odds and ends, like a patchwork quilt, lovingly used to warm different nights and bodies'.[3]

CREATING OUR LIVES

Having said that creativity is something ordinary I may have given you the impression that to live the creative life in the sense I defined above is simple. Find laughter and play in your life and the rest will follow. Well, to some extent I believe this to be true. It may, however, be helpful to describe the experience of creativity and the qualities that may be required of you in order to help you find that laughter. You already have many tools from previous chapters to help you connect with your laughter.

What I want to do with the rest of this chapter is to look at life from the window of creativity. As we put together a jigsaw of the abilities which you need to develop, you will begin to notice that this jigsaw is very similar to other jigsaws we have put together in previous chapters. As we put together laughter and creativity you will discover that only through the development of your emotional literacy will you succeed in leading a creative life. Our emotions are the channel with which our different ways of thinking, G-mode and D-mode, communicate and it is only when all this is working together that we can be truly creative.

When psychologists study creativity, they tend to focus on the few rather than the many, that is, they study artists or 'gifted' individuals to help inform the ins and outs of the creative process. This does not take away from the usefulness of what they have done to help us approach our lives creatively.

The creative process is said to have several stages, which must be gone through though not necessarily linearly. The number of stages varies depending on which books you read. Some divide the process into seven stages:[4]

☺ Desire or motivation

☺ Preparation

☺ Manipulation

☺ Incubation

☺ Intimation

☺ Illumination

☺ Verification.

Others have made life easier for us and have split it into just four:[5]

☺ Preparation

☺ Incubation

☺ Illumination

☺ Verification.

Wallas suggested that it was the interplay of these different stages that led to scientific discovery. He explains the stages in relation to this. A scientist will prepare by carrying out experiments that aim to solve a given puzzle. He will hit a barrier at some point and will leave the problem and go home to sleep on it. He may have to sleep on it for many nights or just one. There is no way of telling or of speeding up this process. You just have to let yourself be. It is sometimes suggested that even verbal descriptions of what you are working on can upset the process. Jonathan Schooler says that 'verbalisation has a very specific effect; it impairs judgement based on intuition.' And that is just the kind of judgement that is at play during the incubation stage. At some point you suddenly and from out of nowhere have an idea that you are sure will take the solution of your problem further. Armed with this you go on to the stage of verification and carry out more experiments to create your elegant solution to the puzzle that you were researching.

The creative process, if it is to produce any output, makes effective use of G-mode and D-mode. You need to be skilled at both to be able to create an amazing meal or discover the endorphin receptor. You have to remember that 'there is more to winning a Nobel Prize than choosing one of the unsolved puzzles of the universe and sleeping on it!'[6]

The affective component, the reason for the exclamation mark in our formula at the beginning of this chapter, is rarely explicitly discussed. However, it is always mentioned in accounts of the creative process as told by creative people. Here is a favourite description: 'I can get carried away completely and I can add time to my own life.'

The emotions that are associated with the act of creation are very strong and very mixed. It is not easy to label them, though it is easy to say that they are intense. I want you to understand that I do not believe it is possible to even start with the preparation stage unless we can deal with our emotions through the reality cycle to some extent. For as long as we are working with our emotions from the magical cycle we will not be able to connect with our creativity in a sustainable way.

Given that we have a basic exploratory drive that allows us to function in a life without script, we can only connect with it through our ability to connect with our emotions in a healthy way. It is this that sustains the creative process and that allows us to move from one stage to another in a fluid and flexible manner. If we do not feel that we have to push away our emotions then we can stay with the discomfort that is inherent in parts of the process that I have just described to you.

It is because we want to avoid dealing with our emotions that we kid ourselves that there is no need to create our lives on a daily basis. Life would be just right if we could make decisions based on the model that we still sell our young people today:

> The model of an ordinary successful life that is held for young people is one of early decision and commitment, often to an educational preparation that launches a single rising trajectory. In fact, assumptions about careers are not unlike those about marriage; the real success stories are supposed to be permanent and monogamous.[7]

The surprise is that even when we subscribe to this approach, we still have to deal with the unexpected. People die, companies close and relocate, illness results when we have too many unresolved emotions stored in our bodies. Bateson says that the problem is that we confuse the kind of problem that life is. We try to fit it into a model of 'if I study for this test then I will pass; if I don't then it's my fault.' We forget that life is such that we find ourselves attending courses the scripts for which are not available, and at times even discover 'that these particular courses are not the ones I signed up for!'

We have a choice: to learn to respond creatively to life or to continue to hang on to the illusion. If we hang on, we get hurt all over again the next time that the world throws a surprise at us. If we learn to respond creatively, we may one day develop wisdom. Bateson defines wisdom as having many ingredients but 'one of the essential ingredients is becoming aware of how many times you have had to change your mind'.

So how can you apply the stages and the emotional aspects of the creative process to your daily life? What is the connection of this with finding your inner laughing place? Knowing about the stages can help you understand that creativity is not just about the moment of illumination, the fulfilment of the exploratory drive which may often have lots of laughter associated with it. To get to that point, there is a lot of 'other stuff' that goes on and this is as much a part of the creative process as the elusive moment of illumination.

You know that incubation takes time, that you cannot rush the process, that it is good for you to prepare for doing something and then have time in-between to just let things be. It is true that the best ideas come to us in the shower when we least expect them and when we have given up trying to find them through D-mode. You also know it's no use just letting things be, of having the moment of illumination and then not verifying your perceptions. If you approach your life from that inner laughing place, and find ways of putting into practice all that you have learned so far in this book then you will have the emotional intelligence that is required to be able to stay with the richness and ambiguity of the creative process. That said, let's look in more detail at what it takes to think creatively.

HOW DO WE THINK CREATIVELY? LEARNING TO HANG OUT IN THE FOG

One of the key themes of creative people, which I have found in my own work with knowledge transfer skills,[8] is that for the process to work they must learn to get out of the way. What they mean by this is that they must learn to switch off D-mode and allow themselves to 'hang out in the fog'.[9] As this switching into G-mode happens there is a feeling of 'being spoken to from behind and being unable to turn around and see who is speaking'. What a wonderful image of creative thought! Ralph Waldo Emerson said this. It describes the sense in which creative people have to let go of the ego and allow themselves to be used almost as a channel, as Thomas Moore puts it, 'to let the soul have its way'. He argues that when we talk about the output of creativity we commit the intentional fallacy. We assume that the artist can tell us what it means.

It is actually quite commonplace for artists to produce but not know the meaning of what they have produced. The explanation comes after the product. This is characteristic not just of artists but also of the way in which all of us think. Michael Gazzaniga has reported extensively on people who have specific brain lesions that stop them from perceiving as we do. When making an unconscious choice of a particular drawing, in response to an unseen stimulus, they will create a narrative that explains the action in a coherent way that has some meaning for the speaker but bears no resemblance to the reality of the experiment. The narrative serves the purpose of reducing the confusion that is generated when we act in ways which we do not consciously control.

We rather create a story at any cost than admit that we don't know. This fear of not knowing is relatively new. It has emerged in our culture since we have started teaching that D-mode is the most valuable way of thinking. Our reliance on D-mode has resulted in the generalisation that it is wrong to not know. And yet, in life we cannot always know. As was said before, not only can we not study for this test, we even get to attend courses we have not signed up for!

We have an expectation of knowledge that is omniscient. Mistakes are not only not expected in our society but they are also punished. Who in their 'right mind' would practise medicine without malpractice insurance? Patch Adams, that's who – a doctor who believes in the patient-doctor relationship as one that has to be based on trust and on the understanding that, even within a framework of excellent skill, mistakes do happen. The courage that he demonstrates in going against the tide of a society which has created a new business area out of suing at the slightest mistake, has to be applauded. He is not, however, an example of a mainstream practitioner.[10]

Here are some Potshots[©11] that make the point with *levitas*:

☺ I keep quite busy trying to conceal the fact that I don't know what I'm doing.

☺ My life is a performance for which I was never given any chance to rehearse.

☺ Correct me if I'm wrong … at your own risk.

☺ Life is the only game in which the object of the game is to learn the rules.

☺ I don't have the solution, but I certainly admire the problem.

So, let's start to design our course on thinking creatively. We will sign up for a few modules that will help us lead creative lives.

EVERYDAY-MAKING 001: DEVELOPING THE ART OF SAYING 'I JUST DON'T KNOW'

In religion they call this 'the via negativa'. Theologians talk about learning to define *what is* by naming *what it is not*. The approach is used to define God, but we can generalise it to define anything in life. So much of what we do daily defies explanation. Yet we insist on providing a narrative for it. Imagine learning to be as comfortable with not-knowing as we are with knowing. So when your neighbour asks 'What are you doing?' you can say, 'I just don't know.' Most of us feel that others will think us crazy if we are unable to explain our actions. Our legal system is based on the assumption that not only are we able to explain, we can also be held responsible for our explanations. Sometimes we can, sometimes we know … at other times we don't. Not knowing is what we need if we are to feel free to be creative in our lives.

Angeles Arrien says that there are four universal addictions, which run deeper in our psyche than the addiction to alcohol, drugs or people. She believes that we are in the grip of an addiction for as long as we don't acknowledge the resource that it has to offer. These addictions are:

☺ Intensity. We can be addicted to intensity when we have not yet learned to express and receive love.

☺ Perfection. We become addicted to perfection when we don't know how to express our sense of being powerful and gifted in a way that is not comparative.

☺ Need to know. We become addicted to the need to know, when we have not accepted our inner wisdom.

☺ Blemish. We focus on what is not working because we haven't yet learned how to own and express our vision for our life.

The one we want to focus on at the moment is the addiction to the need to know. Arrien says:

> These individuals do not like surprises or unexpected events. When we are addicted to the need to know we become masters of control and have strong trust issues. Everything needs to be compartmentalised; information needs to be controlled and relationships strategised. We become dogmatic, righteous, critical and arrogant.[12]

Not a recipe for exploration and play, is it?

We must learn to develop a sense that any understanding that we have is provisional. We need to pay attention to the facts, notice that 'we have been wrong so many times, that we can still be open to learning'. It is this perspective that will help us think in a way that opens possibilities in our lives rather than close them up. Thomas Moore says that in order for us to develop soulful creativity, we need to make friends with our sense of feeling inferior; we need to get closer to our ignorance. So much for the first course we need to attend. What is next?

EVERYDAY-MAKING 002: HOW TO FAIL BETTER

> *No Matter – Try again*
> *Fail Again – Fail Better.*[13]

In order for us to be willing to try out new things in life, we must redefine our notion of success; we must learn to see success in marriages that end, in jobs that are let go, in friends that are lost. Lifetimes of continual redefinition, remember? We have been socialised into believing that this is to be labelled as failure. I read somewhere long ago that failure is nothing more than mis-calculated time. I just did not give myself long enough to get the specific result. Sometimes I may not want the result I get but it is nevertheless a result. As Picasso is known to have said after each painting, 'I know how to paint the next one better.'

If we are to allow our ideas and desires to have a central place in how we live our lives, we must be prepared for 'failure'. We must find strategies that help us deal with criticism and with not fitting in. The Japanese have a proverb that talks about how if a nail stands out it must be hammered back in. This expresses a senti-ment that is present in many societies. We are afraid of transition and change because we do not have the emotional maturity to deal with the affective component of transition. This is the reason for exercising peer pressure on those who want to lead a life that expresses their individuality, their soul.

Thomas Moore uses the image of the fool to explore this issue. He says that we must recognise our fear of appearing foolish and yet 'publish' our ideas and desires. If we learn to enjoy our foolishness we may be able to come to terms with the fact that there will always be someone who knows more than I do, there will always be someone who may not like what I say or what I stand for, and there will always be someone who may be hurt by my actions.

We must become comfortable with our foolishness, feel it, bear it, be it and allow it to be seen. This is necessary, Moore says, because foolishness and failure are an integral part of the creative process. We have the glass whether we like it or not. We can choose what we pay attention to but we must not deny the existence of the glass as a whole. It is both half full and half empty.

EVERYDAY-MAKING 003: IS THIS A PROBLEM THAT I SEE BEFORE ME?

As we learned in chapter 1 the brain has different thinking modes, each suited to different aspects of our experience. We create problems for ourselves when we try to use a hammer to fit a screw and we don't notice that this is what we are doing. All we notice is that we are not getting the results we want, but we don't know what to change in what we are doing.

Guy Claxton talks about the need to learn to distinguish between analytical problems and insight problems in our creative endeavours. An insight problem is the kind of problem that requires you to go through the incubation stage before a solution appears to consciousness, that is, the kind of problem that is suited to G-mode thinking. An analytical problem is the kind of problem that requires logical working out, a lot of preparation in order to get to validation, that is, the kind of problem that is suited to D-mode thinking.

We have to recognise that life presents us with both kinds of problems and that we need to use both ways of thinking to address them. Trying to consciously work out in D-mode how to settle a dispute with my spouse may be like using that hammer. Relationship problems often require that we switch to G-mode and play with the problem over time in order for a resolution to emerge. When we say, 'There is nothing we can do,' we mean that we have reached the limit of D-mode. Time to step aside and engage with G-mode. What this requires of us is that we learn the ability to play with our pain and that we find the way to our inner laughing place.

EVERYDAY-MAKING 004: NOT THE EXPLANATION OF LIFE BUT THE NARRATIVE OF LIFE

Thinking creatively is about understanding the distinction between explanation and narrative. Laughter allows us to access the state of mind where life is about possibilities and not about necessities, not about explaining truth but about telling stories that construct different meanings in our conversations.

> Explanation settles issues showing that matters must end as they have. Narratives raise issues showing that matters do not end as they must but as they do. Explanation sets the need for further inquiry aside. Narrative invites us to re-think what we thought we knew.[14]

We are perceptually lazy. Perception does not construct our world from basic principles each moment. As we saw in chapter 4 what drives our perception is our need to confirm what we think we know. What drives our perception is the set of beliefs and values that we are seeking to prove as true, and not the curious discovering of pattern that we see in children.

A lot goes on in our perceptual system before consciousness. As the sensory data comes in a lot of pre-conscious labelling goes on and will determine what gets into our consciousness. What we take as raw data is a processed four dimensional perceptual sketch[15] that has already been organised within the frame of 'is it positive, is it negative or is it neutral?'

We have access to our sensory data only after that initial sorting. It is certainly not raw and it is certainly not neutral. Guy Claxton's 4-d perceptual sketch means that explanation is the order of the day in our thinking skills. This is how we are able to perceive a stable environment. There is a gap of 350 milliseconds between the body initiating action and my becoming aware that I will initiate an action. A lot happens in this gap that we do not even understand.

The notion that we choose what we do and what we perceive becomes doubtful too when we view things from this perspective. There are those who say that, at most, what we have is 'free-wont', that is, that we can only choose what not to do. And yet … We stubbornly cling to finding 'the right answer', 'the right way of explaining life away'. We do not like the idea that in a very real way we may not be responsible for our actions. Current research in cognition clearly shows that we don't know what it is that we know and we act in the world from a cognitive unconscious that may well be in conflict with our conscious reasons. We discussed the detail of this in chapter 1.

It is this need to jump from explanation to explanation, rather than understand that story-telling may be a better model for our cognitive functioning, that fixes our thinking and stops us from living creatively and keeping in touch with our exploratory drive. Sometimes the story will serve the purpose but we must keep open the possibility that what works today may change in the future.

Our development moves from explanation to narrative when we maintain our connection to our exploratory drive. It moves from one explanation to another when we have lost our sense of how to fulfil it. It is then that we create a belief that 'we just can't change the way we are' and become finite players in the game of life. It is then that an unhealthy shift occurs. If we view a picture, it has a figure and it has a ground. In creative thought the figure should be playing with possibility and the ground should be the output. If we focus on the output, and it becomes the figure, we disconnect from our exploratory drive and lose the only means with which the output can be achieved without even knowing what it is that we have done.

EVERYDAY-MAKING 005: LETTING GO OF THE EFFICIENCY GOD

Allowing the output to truly be in the background is not easy. If we are to do that, we must learn to put efficiency lower than grace in our hierarchy of values. We must understand that efficiency is not always a worthy goal. Efficiency does achieve a task in less time, this is true. And if we can do the same task over and over again we can learn to do it in less and less time. Repetition is about efficiency but not about creative thinking. Thomas Moore puts it beautifully, 'The soul is by nature in movement.' Efficiency is about reducing time. Creativity is about using the time we have, gracefully and with imagination.

Let me give you an example of what I mean. It is based on an article entitled 'Time for sale'[16] which tells about a woman who sells time. Time is portrayed as a non-renewable resource and the article explains that 'in a world of galloping technology, where travelling 3,000 miles is a normal weekly commute for many, time is fast becoming the most precious of all non-renewable resources.' So, we spend our time working more hours than we care to remember but have no time to play with our children. We pay a nanny to do that. We go to Brazil for a two-day meeting, but have no time to cook for ourselves. We pay a cook to do that.

We become, as that article suggested, guests in our own existence. All in the name of efficiency. And we find ourselves at the end of our lives having zombie-like repeated those tasks that we became good at, but having never stopped to ask if this way of spending time was a true expression of our humanness.

Creative thinking requires that we timeshift; that we understand that there are certain things that should not be compromised in the name of efficiency: relationships, taking care of our bodies, nourishing our emotions. If we filter our world through grace and imagination we will attend to the detail of everyday life. We will find creative ways of washing the dishes as well as creative ways of writing that report for work.

> Working to establish a more comfortable style of survival has grown to feel complete in and of itself as a reason to live, and we gradually, methodically have forgotten our original question ... we've forgotten that we still don't know what we are surviving for.[17]

EVERYDAY-MAKING 006: MAKING SENSE OF EVERYTHING

You remember the category game we played in chapter 4? It taught you to do something that is at the core of creative thought. Koestler would say that you are engaging in bissociative thinking when you play that game. We must keep this muscle exercised or it atrophies.

The key point here is that humans look for pattern. If we find it and it works we will use it again and again. Sometimes, we will have found a pattern that does not work but, because it is familiar, we will use it again and again. When you played the category game you may have found yourself thinking, 'That's silly. Of course that category does not exist.' And that is precisely the point. It is unfamiliar. We resist the unfamiliar and must practise making new connections in order to generate new patterns. Only in this way will we be able to replace old, familiar patterns that don't work, with new patterns that will help us get ever closer to our true and unique nature.

This daily 'act of creation' will also have the practical implication that, according to psychoneuroimmunology at least, it may keep you well for longer. So this last course will have you putting together frameworks and ideas that you would not *habitually* put together. If you always do what you've always done, then you will always get what you've always got. The possibility of change and creativity is not part of habitual action. We must practise playing with meaning for no purpose, in order to create new meaning. That is the essence of what the techniques you have learned in the previous chapters will have taught you. Laughter comes from the juxtaposition of 'stuff' that you would not habitually put together in your mind. Reframing and other ways of changing your mind reconnect you with your exploratory drive and flexibility of thought. The importance of understanding play in this context cannot be overemphasised. We will return to this topic later in the chapter.

These are component modules for our course 'Creativity, the art of everyday making'. How do you like the course design? We attend classes everyday in everything we do. We can choose, as Bateson says, to have an attitude of lifelong learning or one of just hanging around for a long time. The one will lead to a fulfilled life; the other will lead to just surviving. I believe that survival is entirely sub-optimal and that we all have a right to express the essence of who we are in the world.

And it is not easy. To live life as a weaving rather than as one 'red thread', means complexity. The dream of the successful linear life has created in us a belief that it is possible to find simplicity in life. I believe that what is possible is two-fold: either the weaving is made up of threads that help me express who I am, or it is some-body else's weaving. Both will be complex, but one will appear simple because I am not emotionally connected to it. If I don't know what is around me, if I use my selective perception to confirm just one thread, then the rest of my energy needs to go to creating a strong divide between my cognitive conscious and my cognitive unconscious to avoid seeing what does not fit in my inner space. This divide will be necessary in order to maintain the illusion.

Healing laughter will not be present in this kind of life. The spontaneity that the creative thinking course breeds will not be available to me. Creativity will be something that others have but is denied to me. In my need for certainty and explanation I will be denying myself the possibility of living out my inconsistencies.

Looking for more laughter in my life is likely to help me focus on the times, however few, where the barriers come down and I allow myself to experience surprise and new perceptions – G-mode and D-mode working together to help me not just survive but thrive.

The paradox of the creative life is that we have to learn to live with tensions – the tension between the vision and the daily chores that are necessary to achieve that vision; the tension between not being afraid of appearing foolish and yet caring for what we do as if our lives depended on it; the tension between the need for habit in order to function in our society and the need to let go of habit in order to develop new habits which may need to be let go of later. It is hard to maintain this sense of provisional understanding, this filter that 'nothing is as it appears to me right now'. It is not always comfortable and that is why we also long for habit, unchanging conditions and monotonous environments. This 'rag-doll' feeling that is expressed in what Robert Fritz calls creative tension is a skill to be developed. We can develop it through our senses, we can develop it through our abstract thought, or we can develop it through learning to feel comfortable putting unrelated words under one heading that 'makes sense to us'.

I have called this skill 'staying on the horns of a dilemma', in my work on the cognitive abilities that enable dialogue in the business world.[18] It is such a foundational skill that it deserves more focused attention. It is similar to our notion of not knowing in module 001. You already can play with your pain. You can work with your beliefs in such a way that you can have a flexible pattern of thought. You are learning how to embed creativity in your daily life. Your ability to stay on the horns of a dilemma is another stop on the route that will lead you to having a 'laughing matters approach' to your life.

STAYING ON THE HORNS OF A DILEMMA

Look at the following drawing:

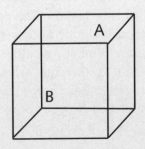

Focus on it and after a little time and with not much effort you will experience the figure change. What do you notice? That there are two possible interpretations of the figure. It is called a Necker Cube and it is a very old example of what psychologists call depth ambiguity. As you look at it you may also pay attention to one interesting fact. Your brain does not mix up the two interpretations but you can select one at a time. Focus on what happens at the moment of the shift between them. There will be an emotional component to your new perception. A sense of 'Oh, yes. There it is again.' You may even find yourself smiling as you play with the ambiguity in a more conscious way.

This is a very simple example of the thesis of this book. We structure our mind the way we physically perceive the world. What we perceive has emotions associated with it and as we have a new perception, we have the sense that we have discovered something new. This leads us to express the emotion outwardly. As our exploratory drive is fulfilled we smile.

This image has another very important quality that is linked to our current focus. It is ambiguous. There is not a right way of seeing it. Both ways are 'right' in the sense that they exist. We can choose which right way to see but the choice takes time. We must stay with it and be comfortable with waiting for 'the other right way' to emerge. We have to hold a certain tension because we find ourselves wanting to see it the right way and soon learn that there is no right way.

This is the essence of what you need to practise in order to develop your ability to hold creative tension. The point is not what is at each end of the tension. It can be discipline on the one side and playfulness on the other or noticing pattern and doing activities that will change the pattern. The point is that there will always be this tension and you need to learn how to direct your attention to use the 'right' interpretation for your purpose at the time. New perception is always there. It is this and it is that – beyond the initial evaluation.

We talked about insight problems earlier. Let me give you an example of this here:[19]

Imagine these are ten coins. You must move only three coins in order to get the triangle to point in the opposite direction. Insight problems ask you to hold the tension between wanting to know and letting your mind wander, what some creative people refer to as an attitude of 'attached detachment'. These problems take time to solve and cannot be worked out logically. Research suggests that the best way of handling this type of problem is to play with it for a while and then go away and let time go by. You will often find that when you revisit the problem, the solution will pop up as if out of nowhere. You will have a small aha-experience. And again you may well find this is accompanied by some kind of emotion. As you see the solution you will find yourself smiling. Or feel angry if you can't see it yet.

We must learn to wait. What we often do instead is try to tackle the problem with D-mode. We start to work it out logically. There is nothing to work out. All the information is there to solve it.

We must learn to wait. It's all about our ability to hold the tension between at least two possible courses of action. Working with a dilemma we often feel uncomfortable and want to resolve it as quickly as possible in order to reduce the discomfort. When we can't, we look for scapegoats. 'The solution is x, if it wasn't for y.'

We can sometimes get to a point where we deny that there is a dilemma at all. This leads us to hold inaccurate information of the world outside, but at least we don't feel the discomfort!

Learning is always about being in transition, from a state we know, to a new state we do not know and feel uncertain about. We often have a lack of clarity as to which are the steps that will get us into the new state and we want to design solutions to close the gap. The extent to which we are able to hold the discomfort and stay with the different possibilities is the extent to which we are likely to find the highest quality solution.

Maybe all that we need to 'do' when presented with an insight problem, and most problems in everyday life are of this kind, is to shift from one side of the dilemma to the other; to keep ourselves in the discomfort zone until a solution can emerge from the data we have available; to look for what is not happening or what is not being said, and doing or saying it as part of our conversations with those around us.

A simple example may be making a decision. Do I move jobs or do I stay? Both are possibilities. No right interpretation. Imagine yourself staying. Run through in your mind a detailed film of this right up to the point when you have made it just fine to stay. And then … Go to the other side. Imagine yourself leaving to go to the new and perfect job, until the film is so perfect that you 'must' leave and go to that new job. And then … go back to that film about staying. And so on and so forth. You get the idea. Each time you will gather more data. Each time you may be closer to a solution, the 'right' thing to do emerging as if from nowhere.

There is a significant amount of research which supports this approach and which suggests that our ability to stay with the dilemmas will generate a better solution. This ability allows us to develop strategies to work with the very essence of learning: the transitions from one state to another. This is similar to the frame-shifting activity you learned in earlier chapters.

Here is a short story that also encapsulates the idea of multiple interpretations being simultaneously available in our experience. It is our beliefs that will determine what we see. This is the reason for making it our task to examine the beliefs that we hold – and make choices as to what is working for us and what is not.

The Right Kind of People[20]

Gone is the city, gone the day,
Yet still the story and the meaning stay:

Once where a prophet in the palm shade basked
A traveller chanced at noon to rest his miles.
'What sort of people may they be,' he asked,
'In this proud city on the plains o'erspread?'
'Well, friend, what sort of people whence you came?'
'What sort?' the packman scowled; 'why, knaves and fools.'
'You'll find the people here the same,'
the wise man said.

Another stranger in the dusk drew near,
And pausing, cried 'What sort of people here
In your bright city where yon towers arise?'
'Well, friend, what sort of people whence you came?'
'What sort?' the pilgrim smiled,
'Good, true and wise.'
'You'll find the people here the same,'
The wise man said.

ACTIVITIES THAT WILL HELP YOU DEVELOP
YOUR ABILITY TO STAY ON THE HORNS OF A DILEMMA

☺ Think Dilemmas, not Solutions

When you need to choose an action in your day, generate multiple possibilities. Get into the habit of having not one way but at least three possible ways. When you find yourself thinking that there is only one way, use this rigid pattern as a cue for giving yourself time to generate more options. If there were more than one way what would it be? Cultivate your ability to have a sense of 'detached attachment' to what happens to you in your life. Hold the tension between both sides of the dilemma in the way we explored earlier.

☺ Exploring Multiple Perspectives – A game with friends

One person identifies a dilemma he or she is currently struggling with, an issue that does not have an obvious solution. Ask three of your friends to act as listeners and two more to act as observers. The person with the dilemma relates the issue to the three listeners. The listeners' role is to understand the person's dilemma, so they may ask questions but only for clarification. The two observers listen and observe and note anything of particular interest.

The three listeners now discuss the issue/dilemma that they have heard between them. The talker just listens this time. The listeners comment on key themes, what was not said, interpretations, and assumptions, surprises they have in response to the story. The person with the dilemma listens to this discussion, as do the two observers. This goes on for a few minutes. Now it's the turn of the observers.

The two observers have an opportunity to discuss what they have heard in the first two rounds – patterns, surprises, what has not been addressed, assumptions etc. The listeners and the person with the dilemma listen to this conversation. The game ends with the person with the dilemma talking about how he or she now sees the problem, having listened to others discussing it – new insights, surprises, questions raised, patterns emerging, etc.

You can then have a few more rounds with other dilemmas or just thank your friends for their help and have dinner!

☺ The Projector and the Screen[21]

This exercise allows you to 'see beneath the surface'. It draws from our capacity to see the world from different viewpoints and helps us understand the 'logic' of apparently opposing views. When we have internal conflicts or dilemmas, it can often seem as if we are going around in circles. Externalising our internal dilemmas can help us gather data in a neutral way and then be in a better position to decide.

Step 1: The projector speaks

This exercise needs you to recruit the help of two friends. You will be the 'projector'. The projector describes a dilemma or a choice which has to be made. Ideally the dilemma should have two alternatives, between which the projector feels caught. The projector describes why this is an issue and explains the two alternative viewpoints.

Your two friends are the 'screens'. The projector chooses which of them will represent each side of the dilemma, as if the projector was reflecting his or her thoughts onto a screen.

Screens should listen for the underlying feel of the position they are being asked to take, embodying the position as closely as possible. Listen out for a key sentence that can start screens off, a sentence that represents each position.

The projector can coach screens until the screen can accurately reflect the projector's mind.

Step 2: The screens speak

When both screens are ready the projector takes a deliberate step back. You are letting the screens have the dilemma for a while. For the next few minutes the screens debate the dilemma. As a screen it is your job to articulate the position you are embodying, not to give advise to the projector. The projector is silent during the debate.

Step 3: The projector reconsiders

The projector reports back on what it felt like to listen. You are all likely to begin to see the assumptions and thoughts of this dilemma as it is suspended in front of you.

☺ The Alexander Technique[22]

We spoke about this earlier. The essence of the technique is that it teaches you, at a bodily level, how to refrain from running to resolution. It teaches to perceive and be beyond the initial certainty that you know what has to be done. They call it inhibiting habitual patterns. It is therefore a way of physically learning to stop thinking habitually, of learning to perceive each moment with a beginner's mind. It is not coincidence that it is used with great success by artists to help gain the state of being needed for performing without end gaining.

☺ Perceptual Ambiguity

10 ♣
Anonymous, "My Wife and My Mother-in-Law," 1888

Can you see both women?

9 ♦
Paul Agule, "Liar," 1987

Can you trust this man? The answer is written all over his face.

Do you see an old woman or a young woman?

What is written all over this man's face?

8 ♥ Anonymous, "Corporal Violet," 1812

Find the three hidden faces.

♠ 8

Can you find the three hidden faces?

K ♥ Salvador Dalí, "The Mysterious Lip that Appeared on the Back of My Nurse," 1940

Do you see a face, or two figures looking at the countryside?

♠ K

A face or two people looking at the view?

These are some of my favourite images. They help to remind me that 'nothing is as it appears right now' and that it is in the constant transition from one right way of looking at things to another that creativity and laughter are found. They are like those stereograms that have become so popular nowadays, those images that on first viewing seem an array of meaningless pattern and then change.

What you need to do with stereograms in order for them to change is maintain this sense of creative tension. You must learn to use focused and diffuse attention. You must learn to wait for the image to appear. You will find your inner laughing place as the image appears and you will feel frustration if you try to apply the wrong kind of thinking to it. D-mode thinking will not get you to see the image that is hidden in the meaningless pattern. But that does not stop people from trying to apply the wrong kind of thinking. Learn to see the images without becoming frustrated by the fact that you cannot force the solution. You will be training your mind to stay on the horns of a dilemma and maybe find more creative solutions to your life problems.

The infinite game of creativity as participation in the world requires that we swim against the stream. In this world that demands shortcuts, clear results and solutions from us, I am asking you to turn your world upside down: allow the output of what you do to stay in the background and let the process of doing it become the figure. It is all there in the image. You simply choose what becomes the focus, depending on your needs. Like in this image by Roger Shepard called 'Egyptian Tête-à-Tête'.

J
♥
Roger Shepard,
"Egyptian Tête-à-tête," 1990

Two girls or one?

♠
ſ

If you focus on the candlestick you will see one girl. If you focus on the girl and 'she' becomes the figure, there is no longer one girl but two! It's all there but you must learn to focus on different aspects *depending on what you want to see*. The relationship between play and the output of play is just like this image. If you play with meaning and with purpose, you will not find creative thinking. If the play becomes the figure and the purpose becomes the background you are more likely to get into the spirit of play.

THE FIGURE: THE PLAY FRAME

> *It is through play that animals and primitive people train their young for the tasks of living. Play is a way of being in the world, a way of coping with the absurdities of the human condition.*[23]

We have spoken about the importance of play in previous chapters. Here I want to focus on play as a means of leading a creative life. As we seek laughter in what we do we also find that we put a frame of play around what we do, even around those things that we label as serious. Something can be important and treated with levity, or important and treated with gravity. Learning to think creatively means that we learn to associate frameworks that would not habitually be put together in our minds. As we learn to be comfortable with this mode of being we will discover a very unexpected payoff. We no longer need to invest energy in keeping our inconsistencies outside conscious awareness. We can hold incompatible worldviews, and this means that we can hold a belief and also notice examples, in our actions in the world, when we are not acting according to that belief. More of our cognitive unconscious becomes available to us.

This can only happen if we are willing to let go of the notion that we play a game to win. We must take on the notion that we play a game in order to keep playing. This is the distinction behind James Carson's book *Finite and infinite games – A vision of life as play and possibility*. Carson says:

☺ To be prepared against surprise is to be *trained*. To be prepared for surprise is to be *educated*.

☺ Death in life is a mode of existence in which one has ceased all play.

☺ Infinite players do not play for their own life; they live for their own play.

☺ The joyfulness of infinite play, its laughter, lies in learning to start something we cannot finish.

The essence of play is not in learning the rules but in learning that we can make the rules and create our own games.

It is easy for me to say that we must play infinite games, rather than play finite games, in life. This is no longer so easy when I think about going to the office on Monday morning and attending that meeting with – my boss. We play finite games because we are afraid of risk and of letting go. Infinite games require that we are comfortable hanging out in the fog of not knowing, that we challenge what we think we know and practise holding the creative tension of opposites.

I will give some specific examples of how to do this in your life should you have the inclination. But first I will tell you about the Surrealist movement and their games. I will then end the chapter with some practical examples of people who are good at the kind of thinking we have been exploring in this chapter, people who are able to use the whole of their life as a pool for making non-habitual associations, people who view their work as an opportunity to create every day.

PLAYING SURREALIST GAMES[24]

The aim of the surrealist movement was to 'exploit the mechanisms of inspiration, to intensify experience', according to its early historian, Julien Levy.

> We have lived for too long in the dreary region of homo
> economicus, our lives shadowed by principles of self-
> interest, utilitarian necessities, instrumental moralities.
> But we are permitted to hope. To revive those great and
> optimistic words of Breton: perhaps the imagination is
> on the verge of recovering its rights. We must welcome,
> as did the surrealists, the re-entry into modern life
> of Homo ludens, the imaginative man at play, the
> intuitive visionary.[25]

As a movement the surrealists were a fascinating example of a group of people who wanted to understand and use creativity. Though they may have had a lot of laughter at their meetings, it was not a specific focus in what they did and created. I offer the following activities for you and your friends to capture the essence of play for the purpose of shaking assumptions and of understanding even further the extent to which a person is a meaning-making machine. We really can make sense of anything. The capacity for narrative has to be, as we said earlier, actively pursued.

Automatic writing

This was the primary method used by surrealists to begin creative activity.

Pen and paper in hand, sit down and begin writing as fast as you can. The trick is to never stop. Don't think about what is appearing on your paper. Just keep going. If you stop, leave a space and immediately begin writing the next letter of the next sentence. You should decide on this letter before you start in order to avoid undue delay. Choose the letter at random and always begin your next sentence with it. You may later choose to edit it. The key is the unplanned associations that create the initial text. The surrealists actually published books of purely automatic text.

For example, 'To what are mutual attractions due? There are some jealousies more touching than others. I willingly wonder in such baffling darkness as that of the rivalry between a woman and a book. The finger on the side of the forehead is not the barrel of a revolver.' By Andre Breton and Philippe Sopault from *The Magnetic Fields.*

Simulation

This is another version of automatic writing. Instead of just writing what comes to mind, this game requires you to adopt 'an active mental state' that is not your own. So you might simulate being, for example, an inmate in prison, and then do your automatic writing from within this state of mind. You might simulate mental illness or any state of mind that may give you a new way of looking at experience and then write your text.

The exquisite corpse and related games

The previous two games can be done alone or in company. This one requires that you have at least three friends who also want to develop their bissociative thinking, or just want to have fun!

Each player gets a sheet of paper and writes a definite or an indefinite article and an adjective which she or he folds so as not to let the other players see what was written. The sheet of paper is then passed to the next player. Everyone writes a noun, folds it and the process is repeated with a verb, another article and adjective and another noun. The game got its name from the first sentence that was constructed in this way, 'The exquisite corpse shall drink the new wine.'

You can play this basic game with more complex sentence structures or with a question and answer format:

- 'What is equality?' 'It is a hierarchy like any other.'

- 'What is a torrent of blood? 'Shut up! Delete that abominable question.'

Or you can play it with an 'if ... then ...' format:

- 'If your shadow's shadow visited the hall of mirrors' 'then the sequel would be postponed indefinitely until the next issue.'

One version that I particularly like is called 'opposites'. One player writes a question or a statement at the top of the page. The next player must write the absolute opposite, whatever it means to him or her, of the sentence and fold the first sentence so as to conceal it from the next person. The paper is then passed on for the next player to do the same. Write the exact opposite of the sentence that is visible and fold the sentence that the previous player wrote. Keep going for as long as you want or until the paper will allow. The wonderful associations that will be made will amaze you.

One into another

At least three people are needed to play this game but if you have a large group of friend it works much better. One player goes out of the room and chooses an object, a person or an idea. While he is out of the room the rest of the players also choose an object. When the player returns he is told the object that the others have chosen. The player must now describe his own object using the properties of the object that the group has given him. The description goes on until the group is able to guess the object that the player had thought of whilst out of the room. It helps to start the description with 'I am an (object)...'

Here is an example, 'I am a hardened *sunbeam* that revolves around the sun so as to release a dark and fragrant rainfall each morning, a little after midday and even when night has fallen.' The word was *coffee-mill!* This example comes from Jane Schuster.

Making text

Take a newspaper magazine or old book. Cut and paste at will. Surrealists used many versions of this basic game to create new text. David Bowie has said that some of his lyrics where produced with this method.

A modern version of this comes under the general heading of 'Poetry Games'. You can buy magnetic poetry kits[26] for your refrigerator or actual games to play poetry slam competitions.[27] In the US there are readings of poetry that has been produced in this way.

This game has an interesting rule called the 'slip of meaning rule'. It states that non-sense sentences are not allowed and that there must be some meaning in the sentence. The other players determine this. What I noticed in playing this game is that the meaning is often given by the way the players read out the sentence concerned. We can indeed attach meaning to any sentence if the non-verbals are just right.

I am fascinated by how much interest people have developed in this kind of word game. It is essentially a way of bypassing D-mode and developing familiarity with putting together non-habitual realms of experience. Maybe we are actually beginning to learn that something was missing from our education ...

Directions for use

This game is a very useful game for learning new associations. Using the format of the directions to be found in everyday household products, d.i.y kits or other ordinary products, apply them to items that would not normally require such instructions. Here is an example by Jean Claude Silbermann, which I have shortened a little:

Death

Its combination of instantaneous and eternal actions ensures that death is harm-less to Man or mammals.

Death does not stain.

Directions:
Remove the self-preserving seal, hold DEATH vertically, valve upward, and apply by pressing the stopper.

For heart complaints: use DEATH centre stage. A few seconds only is sufficient.

For Mystical Ecstasy: use DEATH having placed yourself approximately one meter from clothing, curtains and carpets.

Death is good for you.

Non-toxic

You get the idea. In the book of surrealist games you can also find clear directions for 'the great mystery' and 'the heart'. What would you like to have directions to? Write your own.

The visual exquisite corpse

This is based on the written game that I explained to you above. Surrealists were very aware of the need to sharpen all perception. They used many visual games, but this one is the easiest for you to play with your friends.

Take a large piece of paper, ideally a flipchart pad, and fold it in equal parts. The folds should be horizontal to the proposed picture. Unfold it and begin to make marks on the paper. The first player makes his or her marks in such a way that the marks go slightly over the fold of the paper. The paper is then refolded and passed on to the next player, who begins making marks on the paper using the visible marks from the previous player as the starting point. You continue passing the paper around until it has been refolded back completely. Unfold the whole thing to reveal the masterpiece you and your friends have created.

Would you open the door?

This game needs at least five players to be fun. Players are asked to imagine the following situation: They are dreaming and there is a knock at the door. They open the door and recognise the visitor. They must make an immediate decision as to whether they let him or her in or close the door. What do they decide and why?

Each player announces the visitor and the rest have to write a 'yes' or a 'no' and a brief comment. The comments are read out at the end. The visitor can be famous, alive, dead, someone known to all the players. Use your imagination and discover something about our amazing capacity for rationalisation.

Analogy cards

This is a more complex version of a category game! Get as many of your friends to play as you can. A person known to all is chosen – someone famous, historical, a common friend, someone in the room even.

The aim of the game is to agree a portrait of the person the group has chosen, based on the categories that appear on identity cards. But it is not as simple as that. The categories are given in the form of a set of fixed attributes. What changes is the instantiation of each attribute.

The players write their card. The cards are then shared and discussed until the group arrives at a common portrait that they agree on.

Here is the blank card and an example on Sigmund Freud:

Photograph: An animal	**Photograph:** A star-nosed Mole
Father and mother: Born of the union of	**Father and mother:** Day and night
Place of birth: A geographical location	**Place of birth:** Gizeh, at the foot of sphinx
Date of birth: A historical event	**Date of birth:** 2 December 1814. 10pm
Nationality: A civilisation or culture	**Nationality:** Siberian (paleoartic circle)
Profession: A pastime	**Profession:** Snakes and ladders
Address: A painting	**Address:** The scream of Munch
Height: A vegetable	**Height:** Banyan fig
Hair: A colour	**Hair:** Ultramarine
Appearance: A romantic or legendary hero	**Appearance:** Jason
Eyes: A mineral	**Eyes:** Magnetised iron
Complexion: A meteorological phenomenon	**Complexion:** Midnight sun
Nose: A perfume	**Nose:** Ozone
Voice: A poem	**Voice:** Games of mother and child by Forneret
Distinguishing characteristics: Sexual preference	**Distinguishing characteristics:** Rape
Religion: Conception of the world	**Religion:** Breakdown of frontiers
Fingerprint: Unique signature	**Fingerprint:** Set of scales weighing its own arm

New superstitions

This one is easy. Make up your own superstitions! Keep telling them to your friends and you will discover that if you repeat something often enough people will believe it ...

Some examples from Benjamin Peret:

☺ Cupboards left open bring good luck.

☺ For good luck break your toothpicks after use.

☺ When passing a police station sneeze loudly to avoid misfortune.

☺ Keep the bone of the first sardine eaten every year to avoid money worries.

What is at the basis of a lot of these activities is our ability to make associations that are not habitual. If you need practice doing this as a way of preparing yourself for the more complex activities above, try the simple game below with a friend.

And this reminds me of...

You start to tell a story. As soon as a thought, any thought, pops into your friend's head: Hands up and he or she says 'that reminds me of ...'. You get to hear what your friend's thought is. As soon as a thought pops into your head: Hands up and 'that reminds me of ...' Continue free association for at least ten minutes or for as long as you feel like playing! Pay attention to how you feel afterwards. You are exercising your ability to make connections and that tends to make us feel alive. Our exploratory drive is being fulfilled.

If you want many more games and more fun examples, start with the little book these games have come from. It also has a good set of references to help you find out more about the surrealist movement. I enjoy attending exhibitions of surrealist artists. They remind me of the importance of making new associations. You don't necessarily have to like their pictures. Their work is meant to up-turn your world and make you think.

EVERYDAY MAKING IN ACTION

I mentioned earlier my work on knowledge transfer skills. I carried out a study of individuals who excel at an activity I called 'bridging'.[28] In the terminology we have been using in this book, bridging is the same as creative thought. It is the ability to put two frameworks or contexts or ideas together that would not habitually fit together. My study focused on the activities of individuals who are part of the world of business and large corporations. I wanted to understand the essence of bissociation, in Koestler's terms. The strategy was published elsewhere, but here I want to focus on the role of play in the lives of some of these individuals.

Cognitive semanticists have gathered a great deal of linguistic evidence which suggests that the ability of human beings to understand is dependent on underlying structuring metaphors which are generated from our bodily experience. Eliciting structuring metaphors can be an extremely useful way to explore an individuals sense of identity. In the study I generated some of the operating metaphors in the people I interviewed. For example, one interviewee stated: 'I listen to the radio, or read an article and I say to myself: There must a be a nugget there I can extract.' So, looking for material to transfer into a new domain was, for this person, equivalent to mining for gold. The identity level metaphor could be described as '*I am a gold miner*'.

Other respondents had the following comments:

☺ 'The image has to do with puzzles or jigsaws that when you put them together something else is created, there is a feeling there of elegance of design ... like marketry.'

☺ 'The image I have about my work is not really a straight jacket, it is more like a veil of material and what I do is like poking a few holes in it so that you know people might see through [laugh] ... trying to create opportunities where the fabric tears a bit and there is a glimpse of something else.'

☺ 'In some ways what is important is the resolution and the kind of bringing about of justice in one form of another … so in some ways I'm kind of the inspector Clouzot.'

Among the identity level metaphors which I elicited were: *'I am a bridge builder' 'I am a traveller' 'I am a networker'*. Each metaphor generates particular consequences. Thinking of myself as mining for gold leads me to look for nuggets in the data available to me. I can gather data and use it directly. Thinking of myself as a bridge builder implies that I need to take time to explore what there is in each of the 'lands' which are now separate, to work out how I might build the bridge between them.

Identity was defined in terms of some type of metaphor which would allow the interviewees to use all of their experience as a playground. They did not look for explanation but for narrative and interconnectedness. At work they had to deal with the serious business of helping organisations work more effectively. The way in which they achieved these results was through playfully using all that they did, including gardening and football, as potential material to design conversations with their clients – creativity every day and in every conversation.

Below are some of the responses to the question of what was related to what in their working lives. I had an expectation that they would talk about the serious business of profits and bottom lines and I was surprised. I asked everyone what I came to call 'the unrelated question'. I wanted to learn how they connected 'unrelated' contexts in their life in order to create a bridge from one area of their lives to others.

☺ 'I want to stay in touch with what that "wildness" of me might try at some level to do which I think might just break the boundaries of the institution I am working in. The wildest that I ever got was to suggest to someone senior in a corporation that they write a fairy story. "What about," he said. "I don't know. I just want you to sit down and write one." And he did and he read it to me.'

☺ 'What quite quickly emerges in my mind is a set of words about what might be appropriate in this conversation with my client. I have a list to draw from. My list has: meditation, sport, music, the arts, history, and acting. I have not got as much in my list as I would want. I take from that list what is relevant to the outcome in the form of stories I tell. I would use more hill walking. Sometimes I think that managers could benefit a lot from being alone with only themselves for company in the open space. Philosophy, drawing I am interested in ... and if I can find a way to use it to improve my life then I can offer it to others with my personal experience.'

☺ 'I think that another important issue is that of no boundaries. Why exclude anything? I won't bring something into my teaching in a random fashion. I must first subject it to internal analysis to know where and how it would be appropriate.'

☺ 'What is important is a sense of curiosity, a sense of being interested in life, like a child in a playground, constantly asking questions and testing what you think you know. Learning for me is about increasing the areas of uncertainty. I thought I knew something and then I learn a new perspective: Oh god and I thought I could rely on that! I see my role as a teacher as bringing together different things to play with. Let's mould it, see it from different perspectives, and question it. Which is why I find it frustrating when others will not play. You can practise football on your own ... for a while. You soon get bored if others will not throw the ball back to you.'

☺ 'There is a level at which I can see how things are unrelated, but if I occupy a different space then there is always a relationship.'

☺ 'Having seen the film I would then contextualise the film or think about the film in relation to my life which would include my work and it would be like a ... I sort of imagine it a bit like a ... I was thinking of a spider or a web, so there is the sort of experience of seeing the film ... and you then sort of throw out all these hooks into other areas.'

The essence of what everyone had to offer is that there was nothing in their lives that they could not associate in some way to serve the goal of helping their clients learn and develop. As the quotes above demonstrate, the spirit of play is very much alive in these people. This is not play in the sense of artificially creating games. This is play as life can be playful. Creating links is the essence of the game.

There is an assumption that if you put some thought into it, there is nothing that you could not use in the service of your work. Even a certain clip from *Pulp Fiction*: 'Yeah ... I think ... I'm sure it could. [Laugh] You could ... I think *Pulp Fiction* would be interesting ... There are some scenes in that which, have you seen *Pulp Fiction*? You know when the guy who is Harvey Keitel comes and helps them clean up the mess? I think that would be interesting in terms of crisis management. ... Because what he does is ... he manages to get what is needed done and he's also quite tough with them but he also builds some kind of rapport with them and I think ... I mean there is a bit of a kind of fantasy there and I don't know in a way if it would be good for management because there is a sense when he comes in that he exudes all this authority and charisma and that ... well actually maybe not ... You could say that his reputation goes before him so when they ring him up it is a bit of a last resort but they know that they need him and there is a sense when he walks into the situation, okay he is going to deal with it now, he takes charge, he kind of takes authority. But I mean it would be ... You could show that little snippet as a way of dealing with trouble shooting and the unexpected.'

And this person is also very aware of the role that his emotions play in his ability to be creative in this way: 'I think that the way that I work ... I don't think it is very rational. I think it is very associative; there would be something about the emotion ... probably mine and the emotional experience of the individual or the group I was working with in that moment that would remind me of a film or something I have seen and would strongly suggest that I use it.'

And sometimes it does not work. Sometimes you just need to turn to your ability to fail better: 'The danger is that the connection that I make of it is not necessarily what other people will make with it and also that some of the connections can be quite personal or ... I tend to be guided by the strength of the experience. I just think people were a little bemused by it [my connection of a song with the experience of going back to work] and they did not immediately see what the connection was. Part of the learning was working out the connections. That's true because there were seeds of connections there; it's not as if it was completely disconnected.'

Do you begin to see how it works in practice? I can have the spirit of play in everything that I do. I don't need to become a clown in order to put into practice the ideas in this book. These people are examples of bringing everyday creativity into the work they do, even when the work they do is not about play but about the serious business of helping managers be more effective at what they do: 'I believe that you can learn just as much about the way you dig your garden or you organise your social activities as you can from formal training and development ... so I kind of have a very wide frame of where it is possible to learn.'

Let me give you a few more specific examples by way of closing this chapter.

☺ The man who like quizzes and games – Peter

Peter enjoys games and quizzes. One particular game that he loves is that of 'Dingbats'™.[29] Dingbats consists of many problems that would fit under our heading of insight problems; they are called rebus problems in psychology. You have cards that have a problem and you must find the solution to it. For example:

> ---
> **Reading**
> ---

The solution to this card is 'reading between the lines'.

Well, Peter has to run a workshop on how to deal with change in organisations. Nothing to do with Dingbats, you may say. Not at first sight. Peter goes and selects a number of problems from the game, the solution to which is a sentence that contains some element of the key messages which he wants to give to people in the workshop that he is to run. (See Appendix 1 for the complete set of cards that he used.)

☺ The man who liked films – Mike

You have already met Mike. Mike watches films as a hobby. Some people would say that film has nothing to do with business.

Not Mike: 'If you look at the film, what a good film does, like any work of art, is externalises issues or inner processes and gives people some kind of framework or perspective or maybe another way of looking at their own experience or allows them to tap into aspects of their own experience.'

And this is the essence of what managers in business need to be able to do in order to be more effective. Mike, therefore, has a library of films that he uses when he is working with people in organisations, films which in some way make connections with key messages that he may be wanting to teach.

☺ The woman who liked spheres – Mariana

I like to collect mineral spheres. Yes. I particularly like minerals that contain metals. I hunt for these particular objects everywhere I go in my work.

So what? You may well ask. I once needed a way of managing a group of people who were not able to talk to each other without interrupting each other. I had to find a way for them to listen to each other. I designed a game called 'The talking sphere'. I happened to have a new addition to my collection in my briefcase.

I remembered the concept of the 'talking stick' that American Indians have. Whoever is holding the stick has the word and cannot be interrupted by the others. I did not have a stick but I did have a sphere. The 'Talking Sphere' was born and this group of people used it for a long time to help each other listen. They even bought their own sphere!

☺ The woman who liked stories – Jill

Jill liked to collect stories that were quirky in some way: 'The thing I mainly notice I do is I use stories, funny stories, silly stories, stories about my kids, just tiny moments or tiny stories to illuminate the process. It's got to have that twist to it; it does say something quite important in a funny way.'

Then as she is talking to clients she plays a game with herself to decide when it's the right time to use a story about her child as she is, say, facilitating a board meeting at a particular organisation: 'If it feels like it would be amusing, the time comes when we need to move up and have a laugh at ourselves. It is a sort of skipping, when you decide to jump in or not. Is there a gap? Is there a turning? Do I want to jump? So timing, it's almost unconscious, not thinking. Like skipping. If you did it you just had to do it and not think is this the moment. Almost holding it there until it's time to jump in. And if it doesn't look like it is the right moment, I forget about it and follow the process in a different way.'

Even what happens to you at the supermarket can be used in the serious business of life if you put the play frame around it and are practised in the kind of creative thought we have explored in the last few pages.

The essence of creative thought is complexity. Psychologist Mihaly Csikszentmihalyi suggests that there are 10 key traits in creative people. Such people are:

☺ Energetic and quiet

☺ Smart and naïve

☺ Playful and disciplined

☺ Fond of fantasy yet grounded in reality

☺ Extroverted and introverted

☺ Humble and proud

☺ Masculine and feminine

☺ Iconoclastic and conservative

☺ Passionate and objective

☺ In pain and enjoying what they do.

This set of conflicting traits is a great summary of what we need in order to create our world. We must develop the ability to use both poles, to be comfortable with both poles in each dimension. This is hard and complex work. Laugher may be a way of finding creativity and developing these traits with *levitas* and not *gravitas* – a microcosm for learning how to think creatively and play seriously in the game of our lives.

And finally, here are some of Mihaly's top tips for creativity in everyday life:

☺ Try to be surprised by something every day.

☺ When something strikes a spark of interest, follow it.

☺ Wake up in the morning with a goal to look forward to.

☺ If you do anything well, it becomes enjoyable.

☺ To keep enjoying it you must make it more complex.

☺ Make time for reflection and relaxation.

☺ Shape your space; be in harmony with your surroundings.

☺ Find out what you love and what you hate about life.

☺ Do more of what you love, less of what you hate.

☺ Develop what you lack.

☺ Shift often from diffuse to focused thinking.

☺ Aim for complexity.

☺ Find a way to express what moves you.

I hope that this book has given you ways to do many of these things in your life through a focus on how you can connect with the laughter in your life. May you have your gift of laughter available to you every day of your life. You will find in the pages of chapter 6 a collage of ideas and thoughts and ramblings which help me connect with my inner laughing place. I hope you enjoy them. Good luck compiling your own.

CHAPTER 6

MY GIFT OF LAUGHTER

Life is too important a thing to ever talk seriously about it. Oscar Wilde

What are the purposes that laughter can serve? We have explored many in this little book. Let's sum up:

☺ We use laughter to let people know about who we are and to probe social rules and norms; to push against boundaries.

☺ We use laughter to 'de-commit'. When something is about to go upside down, laughter can help us save the situation by attaching a label of 'not-serious' to it. This is useful to us because in our culture 'not serious' means 'irrelevant' and 'not important'.

☺ We use laughter to puncture the bubble of those people who insist on leading 'the perfect life' with 'perfect people' of which they are a 'perfect' example.

☺ We use it to connect and attract people to us.

☺ We use it to be accepted by groups to which we want to belong.

☺ We use it to stop others from hurting us. If the 'bully' is laughing he is not hurting us.

> *Oh, life is a glorious cycle of song,*
> *A medley of extemporanea;*
> *And love is a thing that can never go wrong:*
> *And I'm the Queen of Romania.* Dorothy Parker

Laughter happens in response to many things and we have explored some of those. We laugh because:

☺ we may feel superior to somebody or something

☺ we perceive an incongruity

☺ we release tension and pent-up emotion.

I have suggested that laughter happens in response to one thing only: the fulfilment of our exploratory drive. All of the reasons just listed have one thing in common, they require that we perceive something, either cognitively or emotionally or both, in a new way. In the terminology we have used in this book it requires that we perceive in D-mode a new morsel from G-mode.

We laugh when the new morsel is one we like, e.g. the release of tension or something that enhances our self-esteem. We cry when the new perception is one we dislike and want to push away, e.g. feeling pain or realising that we are not as perfect as we would like to be. And the emotions often get mixed up. We can sometimes find a way to laugh at ourselves and those who are able to do that are blessed, 'for they shall never be bored'. Or as my wise neighbour puts it: 'Everything in life, girl, has its good part and its bad. People get into trouble 'cause they think they can avoid the bad. They can't. But they will die trying.'

The pushing away process removes us from our ability to have accurate perceptions. It's all there for us to choose. If we don't try to avoid the bad, we can also look for the good within the same situation. We can learn to manage our new perceptions and satisfy our exploratory drive. This is the essence of our creativity and our humanness. By avoiding 'the bad' we also avoid the very process that helps us grow and develop, the perception of new pattern in our daily lives.

The bottom line is:[1]

This is the tragic-comic model of life experience developed by Harvey Mindess. If this is the soup of life, then any event has within it both the tragic and the comic, to a lesser or greater degree.

> *Not only may a humorous view of ourselves help lighten a mood of gloom; not only may it promote an appreciation of the tininess of our individual complaints within the broader scheme of things; it may, I suggest, transform the very texture of our lives, rescuing them both from horror and banality by its refusal to buy into either a tragic or a flatly objective outlook.*[2]

Laughter can help us connect to this creative paradox and we may find that we, briefly at least, can touch 'that place beyond right and wrong' that Rumi talks about in his poems. We can learn to think within the spirit of laughter and play and this can become more than our secret survival technique: it can become our way to wisdom.

J ♥ Anonymous, "Courtship and Matrimony," Late 19th Century

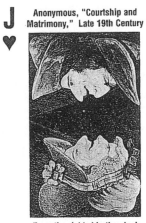

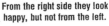
From the right side they look happy, but not from the left.

There is nothing either good nor bad, but thinking makes it so. Hamlet

OF CLOWNS AND CONTRARIANS AND COURT JESTERS AND FOOLS

There is an old joke that shows a man in bed with a big and hairy bug and his wife on the phone talking to his office saying 'Henry won't be coming in today. He's in bed with a bug.' Bissocative thought. Putting together two non-habitual domains of experience.

There is much we can learn about wisdom, by looking in more detail at the image of the fool, in its archetypal sense; the fool as an aspect of our psyche that is and should be an integral part of healthy individuals. One way in which we work toward mental health in our society is through going into therapy. Here is an example of how we could use the image of the fool as a new model against which to measure our therapist:

> Among several models for the psychotherapist consider the court jester. This figure, we are told, made playful comments about the king, his followers, and affairs of state; he punctured pretensions, took an upside down look at human events. Now the patient, it might be said, suffers from gravity. To him life is a burden, his personality a riddle; yet viewed from the outside, he may seem altogether obvious and his problems nothing much. Indeed just because he hurts ... eventually he must find laughter in the midst of his accustomed tears and glimpse his own absurdity.[3]

and Harvey Mindess insists that in order for therapists to be effective they must learn to laugh at themselves. This is not something that therapists are good at doing.

Mindess recounts a story of a presentation he made to a group of psychiatrists and therapists, proposing his view and attempting to show that therapy was 'in various ways an inherently ridiculous enterprise'. Playing the fool in the sense we have discussed and challenging the received view: '... An ominous hush descended in the room. Then the chief of staff – a distinguished psychiatrist whose name only modesty prevents me from mentioning – literally leaped to his feet and exclaimed, "Well, all I can say is, the kind of therapy you practise may be ridiculous, but the kind of therapy we practise here is not ridiculous!"'

Mindess's argument is that if therapists are unable to see the inherent absurdity of life, of which the therapeutic situation is a part, then they cannot help people shift their worldview to a more generative one. It is necessary for therapists to understand that,

'Our profession is nothing if not a spawning ground of foolishness, pretentiousness and paradox – in other words, the very kind of human endeavour that humour was born to feed on.'

This is not a recipe for despair, he suggests, but a recipe for embedding therapy in the realm of common human existence. This awareness can lead to therapists practising their craft as real people and not superior robots: 'We can practise and believe in it as a human enterprise, sharing with all other human enterprises its particular mixture of wisdom, and folly, effectiveness and ineptitude.'

I hope you have enjoyed the example of a therapist as a fool! And that you begin to get a sense of the serious purpose that this archetype can serve in us. I'd like to explore with you a few more examples, not all from our culture. Let's look at one example from the corporate world.

Gordon MacKenzie worked for Hallmark for over 30 years. He had a clear creative role in the company, but found himself often being pulled in to 'the giant hair ball' that was Hallmark. He uses the metaphor of a hair ball for a corporation. The hair ball has a gravitational pull on individuals, a pull towards corporate normalcy. If you succumb to this pull you lose your individuality and become part of the norm. If you don't and you stay you must learn how 'to orbit the giant hair ball', how to stay close to the corporate values and be true to yourself as you challenge the accepted patterns of corporate culture.

In order to survive the pull he set himself up as a corporate fool. Over the years he became known for his creatively rebellious acts. Running a workshop on how to 'Grope' as a vital management skill was one such rebellion. This was meant to teach that the reality of management was not of a 'linear-just-follow-these-steps-nature', but was more like groping for answers and asking yourself constantly, 'What the hell is going on?'

The apex of his career at Hallmark came when he was appointed 'Creative Paradox'. Yes, this was the job title that he negotiated for himself. He takes up the story: 'I did that for three years. The last three years of my thirty at Hallmark I had no job description and a title that had no meaning, and yet they were the most enriching, fruitful, productive, joy-filled years of my entire career. Talk about paradox. Exploit the absurdities and embrace the enigmas. Revel in the power of paradox.'[4]

His job was essentially to support the ideas that employees came up with against the pull of the risk-averse corporate culture. His job title was so alien that nobody knew the extent of his power and therefore assumed that the power was there just in case. So if the Creative Paradox said that it was a good idea, it more often than not got implemented.

MacKenzie's book has an underlying theme that is complementary to our idea of staying on the horns of a dilemma. We must find a way of holding the creative tension, not of eliminating either of the poles that exercise that tension. Total freedom, he suggests, leads to death. Total security leads to vegetating. 'Somewhere between the ridiculous extremes of suicide and vegetating lies the right place for all of us. I've got the feeling that right place is different for you and me. A different place for different times in our lives and different parts of our lives.' Creating our lives is about finding the right place between security and freedom. Being in touch with our fool may give us the courage to let go of the security end bit by bit and find out what else there might be. 'In order to be free to create, we must first find the courage and willingness to let go: Let go of the strategies that have worked for us in the past ... let go of our biases, the foundation of our illusions ... Let go of our grievances, the root source of our victimhood ... Let go of our so-often-denied fear of being found unlovable.'

MacKenzie compares letting go with breathing. It is not a one-off event. If you breathe just once you pass out! 'If you stop letting go your creative spirit will pass out.' His story is a hopeful tale for those of us who work in corporations. It is possible to live the spirit of the fool and maintain our soul and develop wisdom within the security of a corporation. It is 'just' a matter of putting the play frame around our daily meetings, of having access to our fool.[5]

The jester and the clown have a fine ability to hold the tension of opposites, thus creating a balance between security and anxiety, as if their lives depended on it. And, as William Fry states, historically their lives did at times depend on the skill level they possessed: 'To pique the king without causing outrage; to provoke without humiliation; to agitate without inflaming: these are the goals – and the obligations – of the royal fool. A miscalculation of the ingredient, causing disruption of the delicate balance, could be fatal.'[6]

One has to consider the flip side of this risk taking, argues William Fry. In the name of humour the court jester had untold power. He was able to speak the unspeakable, express truths that others were not even able to think, let alone express. He was part of the ruler's innermost thought and experiences. He may even 'be called upon to speak for a ruler those facts or sentiments for which the ruler would not wish to own responsibility.'

We talked in chapter 1 about Victor Frankl's assertion that the ability to find laughter in any situation was a fundamental skill in the art of living. Frankl even created a therapeutic technique called 'paradoxical intention' to make use of his insight. The technique works by creating a paradox in the patient's world. A problem such as shaking in front of an authority figure can get reframed and a task designed to help the patient experience a new meaning. The task in this case was to exaggerate the trembling and show the authority figure 'what a good trembler he was'. The problem is reframed as a gift, the patient asked to live it out as such in his life within the context where it exists.

Frankl's belief is that this technique works because it uses the capacity for self-detachment that is inherent in finding laughter in a given situation. He quotes the following in support of this argument: 'The neurotic who learns to laugh at himself may be on the way to self-management and even cure.'[7]

The fool can tell the truth precisely because the role he has in society is one that is labelled as not serious. The belief that I am challenging in this book is the very belief that lends laughter its power, and herein lies the most fundamental paradox. If laughter is taken seriously, then it matters. If it matters then a legitimate question can be asked: Can it serve its purpose in play and creativity? Maybe not and this is why we find it so hard to take laughter seriously. If we did it would lose the power of communication it now has. The ultimate paradox. I chuckle to myself when I think of this. I hope you can appreciate some of the profound implications of this paradox. Let's now move on. Let's put together laughter and Zen.

Wisdom in Zen is often associated with laughter and the ability to detach. The fool is used as a comparison to a person achieving enlightenment. It is said that such a person has achieved the same kind of 'invincibility that has often been noted on the person of the clown or fool. He cannot finally be conquered, defeated, or killed; for the Achilles heel of Ego, attachment and desire is not there.'[8]

As a final story in this section I would like to introduce you to the contrarians. I came across them in a book by Patty Wotton called *Compassionate Laughter*.[9] She tells of the 'Heyoka' or contrary that the Plains Indians have as spiritual teachers. The Heyoka are expected to start on their path after having a dream or a vision. Their activities are seen as a tool to communicate spiritual truths to the tribe. So what do they do? 'The heyoka are expected to act in ways that break with the traditional norms of the tribe. They perform their activities in reverse: They place lodge poles on the outside of the tipi; they ride horses backwards while shooting arrows over their shoulders; or they sit with their feet up in the air while lying on their backs. These humorous antics … are meant to shatter a person's perception about everyday routines so that they may see things more objectively.'

Non-habitual patterns again. This community has spiritual teachers that help its members stay in touch with the idea that nothing is as it appears right now. Wisdom is gained by challenging habit and there is a worthy role for the fool in helping the community gain wisdom. If creativity in everyday life comes from putting together the unexpected, imagine the impact on your thinking if you were to come out of your house in the morning to find your postman walking backwards opening you letters and reading them! It would make you stop and pay attention, no doubt.

The view that Heyokas represent is that if people can share laughter they become present and can let go of tension and stress. Healing is more likely to happen in this state of mind. Spiritual healers have a very fundamental role in helping the members of their community find their inner laughing place. It is here that health and well being are to be found.

> To become conscious of what is horrifying and laugh at it, is to become master of what is horrifying. The comic alone is capable of giving us the strength to bear the tragedy of existence. Eugene Ionesco

WISDOM AND LAUGHTER

Sandra Steingraber in *Living Downstream* explores the simple story of those river dwelling people who perfected the art of fishing out the bodies that kept floating by and got really good at reviving them too. Yet they never walked upstream to find out who was pushing them in. She uses this story to talk about the environmental causes of cancer. I want to use it to help us realise that we also need to take a walk upstream to find out the causes for the lack of well-being in our lives generally.

An important key, I believe, lies in the way our culture devalues laughter and the kind of playful thinking that comes with it. We must learn to change this trend and come to terms with the fact that this way of thinking takes time and cannot always be focused on a known result. We must stop working and start plerking.[10]

Living Downstream's title was inspired by a parable about a village overlooking a beautiful river. The residents who lived here began noticing increasing numbers of drowning people caught in the river's swift current and so went to work inventing ever more elaborate technologies to resuscitate them. So preoccupied were these heroic villagers with rescue and treatment that they never thought to look upstream to see who was pushing the victims in. This book is a walk up the river of human cancer. Prologue to Living Downstream[11]

To put together the realms of laughter and wisdom is not as far fetched as it may at first appear. As we saw in the previous section, it is nothing new. There are many examples in our culture, in other cultures and through history of the fool in one form or another representing the paradox of wisdom. If you still need convincing you may like the following quote from a very respected Tibetan Lama: 'Since everything is an apparition perfect in being what it is, having nothing to do with good or bad, acceptance or rejection, one may well burst out in laughter.'[12]

The fundamental point here is that 'A person may be most ready to laugh when every pretence about reality vanishes.' For as long as we have to direct our attention to keeping up appearances we are not free to truly connect with that laughing place and burst out in laughter, like the lama. Or a Woody Allen might put it:

What if everything is an illusion and nothing exists? In that case, I definitely overpaid for my carpet.

The Koan of the upside circle encapsulates the essence of how laughter-as-world-view can be a practical guide to life. In a wonderful little cartoon book called *The upside down circle*, the main character, Unk, is given the task of searching for the upside-circle.

As you struggle to imagine an upside down circle in your mind without looking for explanation but focusing on the narrative, you may find yourself discovering a different quality of mind, one where barriers between existing categories break down and one where you 'discover' seeing for the first time. I go back to the upside down circle whenever I need reminding that G-mode is important and that, in the picture of life, the figure is the play frame and the output only the ground. It is up to us how we focus our attention.

The reason that we have to struggle with the giant hair ball of our society is that we have been strongly socialised to separate work and play: 'At school we separate work time from play time. The predominant western religions are built on a code of 'Thou shalt not ...' The image we hold when we refer to the Protestant work ethic is one of dour and serious effort – a world in which fun has no part to play.'[13]

Our society does not trust pleasure as a guide and this distrust has been taught to us through myth, law and the beliefs that we learn from our parents and other significant adults. Steve Tarpey goes on to say that fun, in the context of the corporate world at least, is implicitly cast alongside incompetence and that the unconscious belief that drives our behaviour at work is that we must remove fun from the serious business of our business life. And yet when asked what motivates us at work we reply 'fun, of course' – a clear example of the way in which our actions can, and often are, derived from inconsistent beliefs, as I explained in previous chapters.

These beliefs about the distance between play and work run deep in our collective psyche and we must be aware of the impact that history and the norms of our society will have in our attempts to create a new world-view. It will be hard. But,

Be realistic. Demand the impossible!

A FEW LAUGHTER 'POST-ITS'®

We know that laughter is good for us. We know we feel better after we laugh. As we allow life's pressures to take hold, we forget what we need to do to allow laughter back in. When I don't want to forget something, I write it on a Post-it® sticker as a memory jog. As we come to the end of our time together I want to leave you with a few of my favourite post-its®:

☺ The glass is both full and half-empty.

☺ Pain and joy are always contained in any one experience; it is just a matter of what we choose to find within it at any given moment.

☺ This is just not funny ... but it could be.

☺ The extent to which I can cry will determine the extent to which I can laugh.

☺ Laughter is the shortest distance between two people.

☺ You can't laugh and think at the same time; laughter is thinking below the neck!

☺ The fact that something is not serious does not mean that it is not significant.

☺ What is funny about us is precisely that we take ourselves too seriously – R. Niebuhr

☺ What else could this mean to me right now?

☺ Our heads are round so that our thoughts can fly in any direction – Francis Picabia

The pages that follow are from my own treasure chest. I keep two files that I take to work with me always. One is called 'the funny side' and the other is called 'the serious side'. I dug into 'the funny side' to offer you some final morsels of what makes me laugh. Enjoy.

They are in no particular order and have been included for no particular reason, just the way life is sometimes!

My Morning Prayer

God grant me the serenity to accept the things I cannot change
The courage to change the things I can
And the wisdom to hide the bodies of those people I had to kill
today because they pissed me off.

VIRUS ALERT

> If you receive an e-mail with a subject line of
> "Badtimes," delete it immediately WITHOUT reading it.
> This is the most dangerous E-mail virus yet.

> *It will copy all your personal information (SS #, bank*
> *accounts, credit cards) and post them on a semi-legal web*
> *page for sale.*
>
> *It copies all the addresses in your e-mail address list and*
> *sends obscene messages from you.*
>
> *It changes passwords for all protected files and*
> *applications. It will – re-write your hard drive. Not only*
> *that, but it will scramble any disks that are even close to*
> *your computer.*
>
> *It will recalibrate your refrigerator's coolness setting*
> *so all your ice cream melts and your milk curdles.*
>
> *It will demagnetise the strips on all your credit cards,*
> *reprogramme your ATM access code, screw up the tracking*
> *on your VCR and use subspace field harmonics to scratch*
> *any CDs you try to play.*
>
> *It will give your ex-boy/girlfriend (ex-husband/wife)*
> *your new phone number.*
> *It will mix antifreeze into your fish tank.*
>
> *It will drink all your beer and leave its dirty socks on*
> *the coffee-table when there's company coming over.*
>
> *It will hide your car keys when you are late for work*
> *and interfere with your car radio so that you hear only*
> *static while stuck in traffic.*
>
> *It will give you nightmares about circus midgets.*
>
> *It will replace your shampoo with Nair and your Nair with*
> *Rogaine, all the while dating your current boy/girlfriend*

> (husband/wife) behind your back and billing their hotel
> rendezvous to your Visa card.
>
> It will seduce your grandmother. It does not matter if
> she is dead, such is the power of Badtimes.
> Badtimes will give you Dutch Elm disease.
>
> It will leave the toilet seat up and leave the hairdryer
> plugged in dangerously close to a full bathtub.
>
> It will not only remove the forbidden tags from your
> mattresses and pillows, it will refill your skim milk with
> whole.
>
> It is dangerous and terrifying to behold. It is also a rather
> interesting shade of mauve.
> These are just a few signs. Be afraid. Be very, very afraid.
> ————————-End of Original Message————————

From the ridiculous to the sublime – it's all contained within the same soup of experience and it is okay for you to choose what to focus on at any given time. Serious frames and play frames are valid filters for life. What matters is whether it is you or other people who determine the way you look at your own life. If it is you, you have genuine choice. If it is others, you may find yourself at the end of your life with somebody else's life flashing in front of you!

> Today I wield a wider brush. And I'm swooping it through the sensuous goo of cadmium yellow, alizarin crimson or ultramarine blue to create the biggest, brightest, funniest, fiercest damn dragon that I can. Because that has more to do with what is inside of me than some prescribed plagiarism of somebody else's tour de force.

The above is a plea from the heart by Gordon MacKenzie for all of us to manifest our uniqueness in the canvas of life. Easy to say, but making a commitment to do this does put us in a dilemma, one that maybe we are meant to stay with throughout our lives – one that we must befriend if we are to become all we can be.

The dilemma

To laugh is to risk appearing a fool

To weep is to risk being sentimental

To reach for another is to risk involvement

To expose feelings is to risk rejection

To place your dreams before the crowd is to risk ridicule

To love is to risk not being loved in return

To go forward in the face of overwhelming odds is to risk failure

But risks must be taken, because the greatest hazard in life is to risk nothing

The person who risks nothing, does nothing, is nothing

He may avoid suffering and sorrow but he cannot learn, feel, change, grow or love

Chained by his certitude he is a slave

He is forfeiting his freedom

Only a person who takes risks is FREE.

Leo Buscaglia

And back to the ridiculous again with another favourite e-mail:

ACTUAL NEWSPAPER HEADLINES FROM 1998

Include Your Children when Baking Cookies
SOMETHING WENT WRONG IN JET CRASH, EXPERT SAYS
Police Begin Campaign to Run Down Jaywalkers
Safety Experts Say School Bus Passengers Should Be Belted

Drunk Gets Nine Months in Violin Case
Survivor of Siamese Twins Joins Parents
IRAQI HEAD SEEKS ARMS
Is There a Ring of Debris around Uranus?
Prostitutes Appeal to Pope
PANDA MATING FAILS; VETERINARIAN TAKES OVER
BRITISH LEFT WAFFLES ON FALKLAND ISLANDS
Eye Drops Off Shelf
Teacher Strikes Idle Kids
Clinton Wins on Budget, But More Lies Ahead
Enraged Cow Injures Farmer with Axe
PLANE TOO CLOSE TO GROUND, CRASH PROBE TOLD
Miners Refuse to Work after Death
JUVENILE COURT TO TRY SHOOTING DEFENDANT
Stolen Painting Found by Tree
Two Sisters Reunited After 18 Years in Checkout Counter
Killer Sentenced to Die for Second Time in 10 Years
NEVER WITHHOLD HERPES INFECTION FROM LOVED ONE
WAR DIMS HOPE FOR PEACE
If Strike Isn't Settled Quickly, It May Last a While
COLD WAVE LINKED TO TEMPERATURES
Deer Kill 17,000
Enfields Couple Slain; Police Suspect Homicide
Red Tape Holds Up New Bridges
Typhoon Rips Through Cemetery; Hundreds Dead
MAN STRUCK BY LIGHTNING FACES BATTERY CHARGE
NEW STUDY OF OBESITY LOOKS FOR LARGER TEST GROUP
ASTRONAUT TAKES BLAME FOR GAS IN SPACECRAFT
Kids Make Nutritious Snacks
Chef Throws His Heart into Helping Feed Needy
ARSON SUSPECT HELD IN MASSACHUSETTS FIRE
Ban On Soliciting Dead in Trotwood
Local High School Dropouts Cut in Half
NEW VACCINE MAY CONTAIN RABIES

And a couple of little gems for the dull days at the office:

RE: PHRASES USEFUL IN THE WORKPLACE
I think there's something here for everyone.
> 1. *Thank you – we're all refreshed and challenged by your unique point of view.*
> 2. *The fact that no one understands you doesn't mean you're an artist.*
> 3. *I don't know what your problem is, but I'll bet it's hard to pronounce.*
> 4. *Any connection between your reality and mine is purely coincidental.*
> 5. *I have plenty of talent and vision; I just don't care.*
> 6. *I like you. You remind me of when I was young and inexperienced.*
> 7. *What am I – flypaper for freaks!?*
> 8. *I'm not being rude. You're just insignificant.*
> 9. *I'm already visualising the duct tape over your mouth.*
> 10. *I will always cherish the initial misconceptions I had about you.*
> 11. *It's a thankless job, but I've got a lot of Karma to burn off.*
> 12. *Yes, he is an agent of Satan, but his duties are largely ceremonial.*
> 13. *No, my powers can only be used for good.*
> 14. *How about never? Is never good for you?*
> 15. *I'm really easy to get along with once you people learn to worship me.*
> 16. *Your idea seems reasonable ... Time to up my medication.*
> 17. *I'll try being nicer if you'll try being smarter.*
> 18. *I'm out of my mind, but feel free to leave a message ...*
> 19. *I don't work here. I'm a consultant.*
> 20. *Who, Me? I just wander from room to room.*
> 21 *My toys! My toys! I can't do this job without my toys!*
> 22. *It might look like I'm doing nothing, but at the cellular level I'm really quite busy.*
> 23. *At least I have a positive attitude about my destructive habits.*

> 24. *You are validating my inherent mistrust of strangers.*
> 25. *I see you've set aside this special time to humiliate yourself in public.*
> 26. *Someday, we'll look back on this, laugh nervously, and change the subject.>*

RECOGNISE THIS SCENARIO?[14]

THE PLAN

In the beginning was the plan.
And then came the assumptions.
And the assumptions were without form.
And the plan was without substance.
And darkness was upon the face of the workers.
And the workers spoke among themselves saying,
'This is a crock of shit and it stinks.'
And the workers went to their supervisors and said,
'It is a pail of dung and we can't live with the smell.'
And the supervisors went unto their managers saying,
'It is a container of excrement, and it is very strong,
such that none may abide by it.'
And the managers went unto their directors and said,
'It is a vessel of fertiliser and none may abide its strength.'
And the directors spoke among themselves saying to one another,
'It contains that which aids plant growth and it is very strong.'
And the directors went to the vice-presidents saying unto them,
'It promotes growth and it is very powerful.'
And the vice-presidents went unto the president and said,
'This new plan will actively promote the growth and vigour
of the company with very powerful effects.'
And the president looked upon the plan and saw that it was good.
And the plan became policy.
And that, my friends, is how SHIT happens.

And a few real requests at a reference library in a Borough of London I work with:

☺ I want the Monday edition of *The Sunday Times.*

☺ Have you got tomorrow's edition of the *Evening Standard?*

☺ Where do I find that picture of the Dalmatian against the spotty background?

☺ 'I want a book on a Volvo.' 'You mean a manual?' 'No, it's an automatic!'

☺ Could you give me the opening times of the Gentlemen's toilets as I have an important appointment there.

☺ 'I'm doing some local history research on a person.' 'Who is it?' 'I'm afraid I can't tell you – it's top secret.'

And if after all this you still feel the need to practise laughter in a formal setting, and for laughter's sake, you might consider starting your own 'Laughter Club'.

AN INDIAN LAUGHING CLUB WITH HEALTH BENEFITS

Summarised from a story by Sumit Sharma, entitled 'Stressed? Inhibited? Grumpy? Join the (Laughing) Club, Indians Say', in the Wall Street Journal (Dec 9th '96) monitored for the Institute by Roger Knights.

Endorsement of the proverbial wisdom about laughter's health-giving properties arrives from Bombay, where a local doctor has instigated a trend for medicinal 'laughing clubs'. Dr Madan Kataria, who propounds a mirth-inducing posture technique derived from yoga, set up the Priydarshini Park laughing club in 1995. Since then, more than 100 laughing clubs have been rapidly established after his model right across India.

Members of the clubs meet in groups of up to 50, where after limbering up and breathing exercises, they egg each other on into extended bouts of hilarity.

Chhaganbhai Seth, 72, was told by his grandchildren that he was noticeably less grumpy after four months of laughing practice.

Practised gigglers learn how to produce a repertoire of different styles of laughing, and the health benefits claimed are numerous. As well as loosening inhibitions and boosting self-confidence, Dr Kataria says it is also good for breathing, as an aid to giving up smoking, and can alleviate hypertension, arthritis and migraine.

Update on laughter therapy from an article by Tony Allen-Mills in the Sunday Times *(Jan 3rd '99).*

In 1998 Kataria organised a World Laughter Day at the Bombay Racetrack and 10,000 people turned up. 'We all had a jolly good laugh,' he said. While he has been formalising his laughter techniques, American research has shown that laughing lowers blood pressure, reduces stress hormones, and boosts immune functions. It also triggers the release of endorphins, the body's natural painkillers, and fosters general spiritual sunniness. All this has encouraged American doctors to prescribe laughter to gloomy patients.

A new film, *Patch Adams,* stars Robin Williams as a doctor who makes cancer patients laugh. 'It sure as heck helps to have movies like this,' said Robert Cicco of the American Association for Therapeutic Humour. One Pittsburgh hospital provides a 24-hour television channel called Humour Helps Healing, and humour therapists have formed the Carolina Humour and Healing Association (HaHa). Hospitals all over America are studying 'humour intervention' programmes – some including Kataria's exercises.

You can rate how well you like this idea. Click 0-10 below and press the Submit button.

● ● ● ● ● ● ● ● ● ● ●
Bad Idea 0 1 2 3 4 5 6 7 8 9 10 – Great Idea

Submit

As of 06/03/99, **89** people have rated this page with the overall rating (0-100%) of: **93%**

E-mail comments or new ideas to the Global Ideas Bank at *rhino@dial.pipex.com*

The *Global Ideas Bank home page* is at
http://www.newciv.org/GIB/

Order the publications on which the Global Ideas Bank is based.

I created my own Laughter Workout inspired by this laughter therapy. We start the second day of my workshop with it. The aim is to learn to laugh for no reason at all. We laugh for 30 minutes unconditionally. We laugh as Dr Kataria suggests 'because we can, not because of some outside stimulant. We want to liberate laughter from conditions.' It is a delightful way to start our day. Look into Appendix 3 if you want to get a framework to help with the creation of your own laughter workout.

AN ALMOST FINAL AND SERIOUSLY FUNNY WORD

I want to introduce you to some images that have fascinated me of late. They come from an organisation called Adbusters, and contain the kernel of all that we have learned in this book in one simple image. They are called 'spoof-ads' and use our selective and predictive perception in order to drive home, using *levitas*, serious messages about the downsides of our developed world. Here are three of my favourite images. Visit them at:

www.adbusters.org

as they update their information regularly.

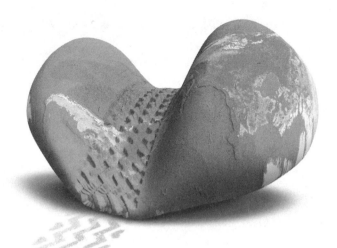

What was that bump?

WHEN ONLY A FEW WORDS SUFFICE

I want to leave you with one of my favourite paragraphs. Of all the conversations I have had and all the books I have read in preparation for this little book, I believe that John Morreal has put it most simply and elegantly:

For the person who can laugh amusement is valuable not only as a means but as an end, just as any aesthetic experience is. He will not only be amused more often than the serious person, but will enjoy moments of amusement for their own sake. Such a person will often have practical concerns, of course, and will work as well as play. And yet he will not be locked into a practical frame of mind – even while working he will retain his ability to occasionally step back and laugh at the incongruities of life which we encounter every day. This involves flexibility and openness. In part this flexibility comes from the realisation that what is important is relative to the situation someone is in and to his point of view.

Nothing **is** *important simpliciter*[15]

In realising how much laughing matters in our lives we may also discover that its importance lies in it not mattering. We might as well laugh.

APPENDIX 1

PETER'S DINGBATS ABOUT CHANGE

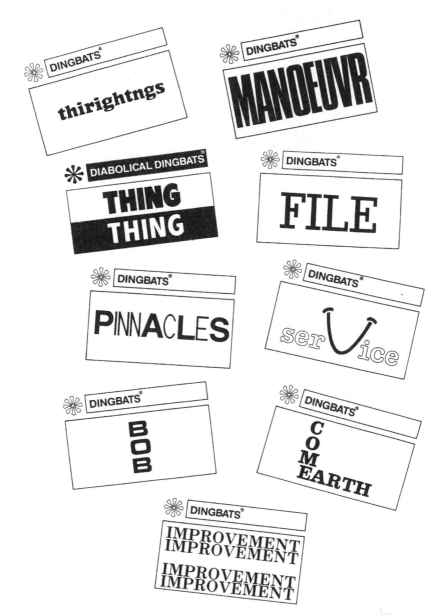

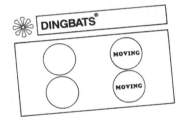

APPENDIX 2

SHOULD WE BE WORKING OR ... LARKING?

At the end of one of my workshop on the very serious topic of how much 'Laughing Matters' in our life, one of the participants came up to me to me and said;

> You talk about combining laughter and work, I wonder if that is part of the origin of the expression 'larking about'? Have you heard it? The interesting thing is that we use it at work a lot. If anyone is having a laugh we tell him or her to stop larking about, don't we?

I don't know the etymology of the word, but I liked his idea. This short article will give you a short answer to the question of the title. I must, however, reveal my bias before we start: I believe we should most certainly be larking about as much as we have the courage to!

Roffey Park Management Institute asked me, a few years ago, to offer a workshop on the topic of laughter at work. I planned for a small gathering of 10 people, but over 60 people actually attended on the day! Many senior managers and directors of large organisations gathered to explore the relationship between laughter and work. This was the start of my journey into becoming 'the laughter expert'. Since that tentative first step many workshops have run, a book has been written and I have had more media exposure than I feel comfortable with.

But enough of my personal story. I now want to turn to the question of the title of this short article. I want to start by exploring what work means to us and move on to talk about how laughter and play have no place in our traditional view of work. I will end with my answer as to why laughing matters in our life, not just at work, and give you some key guidelines for connecting with what I call your inner laughing place – that place within all of us that helps us deal with stress in a way that keeps us real. Like the Velveteen Rabbit of the children's tale, whose mission it was to learn to be real.

You already know that laughter is contagious, that laughter involves all of you and that, sometimes, you can laugh until you cry. Laugher happens when we play, but should not be part of serious work.

WHAT IS WORK? WHAT IS PLAY?

We take work seriously. Play is not serious. Play is for children. Work is for adults. If we are playing we are not working and the two should never mix. For if we play at work we cannot be thorough in our work and we are most surely being unprofessional. Or are we? Let's talk some more about the notion of play and its power. When we joke about the misfortunes of other people or ourselves, we laugh at a victim. But in play the victim is not real, but virtual. If we say, 'It's just a joke,' this means it is not real. We are putting a play frame around something painful, as in the case of jokes about national tragedies. William Fry actually defines humour as play,

> first, humor is play. Cues are given that this, which is about to unfold, is not real. There is a 'play frame' created around the episode.

From this we could argue that there is no hurtful humour. If we put a 'play frame' around it, any topic can be used to help us laugh. To some extent this is true. What is missing from this equation is permission. Putting a play frame around some awful event at the office will help us deal with the awful event so long as all the parties concerned have agreed that 'this is play'.

A lot of the laughter that happens in organisations is what I label hurtful laughter; there is no permission. We tease and ridicule others under the very convenient heading of 'What is the matter with you? Can't you take a joke?' With that the victim is caught, unhappy about being picked on without permission but unable to say anything for fear of being labeled a spoilsport. Do you recognise any of this?

When there is permission we can have the kind of laughter that helps us deal with stress. We can put a genuine play frame around work and benefit from all its qualities:

☺ It does not matter.

☺ It is not important.

☺ We can experiment and fail. Try again and fail better.

☺ We can play with meaning for no purpose.

☺ The end goal is in the background.

☺ What matters is to keep the game going.

If work is play then we can achieve that most fundamental of all work skills: we can be creative. When you give a monkey a problem to solve and it expects a reward, it takes longer to solve the problem than when it is just messing around with the problem! Humans are not that different. If we can think about our work as play we can free up our imagination and find ways to find laughter in our day even when the content of our work may be repetitive.

LAUGHING MATTERS

Laughter is important because:

☺ it releases tension

☺ it gives us perspective

☺ it helps deal with adversity

☺ it give us a mental time-out from everyday stress

☺ it is a drug-free way of re-balancing our body and countering the harmful effects of stress.

That laughter helps us deal with stress mentally is something that most of us do not need to be convinced about. The problem is that at the most stressful times we forget about this important survival technique. We judge *that* time to be inappropriate for laughter. *This* is not funny. *This* is serious. Well, next time you find yourself making that particular judgement, bear in mind what I'm about to tell you about the connection between laughter and stress.

Stress creates unhealthy physiological changes. The link between stress and high blood pressure, muscle tension, a suppressed immune system, and many other changes has been clearly demonstrated over the many years of research on this topic. We also appear to have proof that laughter has just the opposite effect on our body. Researchers have shown that the experience of laughter lowers cortisol levels, increases the amount of activated T-cells, increases the number and activity of natural killer (NK) cells ... And so it goes on. In short, laughter stimulates the immune system, offsetting the effects of stress. Let's look at these effects in more detail:

☺ During stress, the adrenal gland releases corticosteroids that are quickly converted to cortisol in the blood stream. High levels of these have an immunosuppressive effect. Research has shown that laughter lowers cortisol levels and protects our immune system.

☺ NK cells, a type of immune cell, attack viral or cancerous cells. They are key in the prevention of cancer. Cells in our bodies are constantly changing and produce potential carcinogenic cells. A healthy immune system mobilises these NK cells to destroy abnormal cells.

☺ T cells are activated in laughter, which provide lymphocytes that are ready to deal with a potential foreign substance.

☺ In 1987, at the State University of New York, it was found immune activity was lower on days of negative mood and higher on days with positive mood. A positive mood can be measured by amount of laughter activity.

☺ Other researchers at Western New England College found that people showed an increased concentration of immune substances after viewing a funny video.

☺ Herb Lefcourt, from the University of Waterloo, found that subjects who tested strong for appreciation and utilisation of humour had higher levels of a particular immune substance after viewing a funny video than subjects who tested weak. They laughed more and hence the levels of immune activity were higher.

I could go on. The research that is available about the beneficial effects of laughter supports our intuitive understanding that laughter is important beyond doubt.

If laughter is so good for us, and thinking of work as play can give us more ways of finding laughter in our daily grind, then we should be able to go into any office and notice employees laughing and playing as they do their work. We should indeed all be larking about as it is good for our health and our creativity.

But we are not.

HOW DO WE STOP OURSELVES FROM LAUGHING?

We stop ourselves from using laughter more because of that judgment I talked about earlier. It is not appropriate to laugh at work. If we laugh and play then we are not professional. Let me tell you about some of the beliefs that lurk below the simple comment 'Can you keep the noise down? We are trying to get some work done here.'

LAUGHTER BARRIER 1: 'WHY ARE YOU LAUGHING? IT'S NOT THAT FUNNY'

We stop ourselves from laughing by making the assumption that we must have a conscious reason to laugh. The reality is that most conversational laughter is spontaneous. Most laughter is conversational and not in response to humour. Thus we can say that if we focus our attention on increasing the kind of laughter that naturally occurs in conversation we are helping our body remain healthy.

Let's look at the work of one researcher who focuses on conversational laughter. Robert Provine has found that most laughter has little to do with jokes or funny stories. Most of the laughs in his studies followed mundane statements such as 'It was nice meeting you, too' or, 'Can I join you?', which did not meet 'traditional standards for humour'. Only 10 to 20 per cent followed a punch line.

Mutual playfulness, in-group feeling and positive emotional tone mark the social settings of most naturally-occurring laughter. One of the key features of natural laughter is that it occurs in speech and is not randomly spread throughout the speech stream. It has a clear pattern. For example, Provine says, the speaker and the audience seldom interrupt the phrase structure of speech with laughter. The strong and orderly relationship between laughter and speech is similar to punctuation in written communication.

Provine's study reveals other clues about laughter in human communication. An interesting but counter-intuitive finding is that the average speaker laughs about 46 per cent more often than the audience. Find yourself an audience and just talk. Conversational laughter seems to account for most of adult laughter and it is the kind of laughter that we should be encouraging in ourselves and others to gain the physiological and psychological benefits we have discussed.

LAUGHTER BARRIER 2: 'THAT'S ENOUGH! LET'S GET BACK TO WORK!'

If we are laughing we are not working. Laughter not only helps us deal with stress and keeps our immune system healthy; it also oxygenates our bodies. If we laugh while we work, we are more likely to get better results for ourselves and for our organisation – to say nothing of the higher motivational levels of a work force that feels free to lark about as part of working towards the goals of the organisation. I recently heard from a department head that gave an employee a bonus for 'increasing the morale of the team'. When asked what the employee did, he said, 'She has a way of getting us all to laugh when things are going terribly wrong. This helps get out of problems quicker and work better together as a team.'

I wish that more managers were so enlightened. Compare this instead with the recent example of an employee who was dismissed from her job for using the Internet to book her holiday. No play in that workplace! I wonder what their turnover and absenteeism levels are.

Stress makes people ill. Those of us who run organisations must remember this. We have a duty of care towards our employees. We should encourage constructive ways of dealing with stress. Laugher is one of those ways when it occurs naturally between people and is not forced upon them.

We must ask how can we support it, not how can we 'make' them laugh more. You cannot 'make' people laugh if you want the laughter to be health giving. You can only encourage natural laughter by living your work day as if laughing matters to you. You have to become the change that you want to see around you. If others see you use laughter constructively, they will learn to do more of it in their own working lives. But most of all, if you are in a senior position, they will learn that they have permission to do what comes naturally.

You will have more motivated, healthier and creative employees. And people need both their health and creativity in order to cope with an ever changing environment and ever increasing demands. Next time you find yourself larking about remember that laugher keeps us healthy and creative.

But why wait until laughter finds you? Find below some ways in which you can find it more often in your working life. If you want to learn more ways come to one of my workshops! We play very seriously for two days and you leave with a mental bag full of techniques to find more laughter in your day. The key message is that you have to learn to be laughter independent, free from the barriers that you have unquestioningly taken on from a working culture that requires that laughter be associated with inefficiency and trivia. You can choose to associate laughter with efficiency and creativity.

Leaders who intuitively understand the importance of laughter use it as a tool for motivation and enhanced performance. A recent article in the *Financial Times*, 'Fun at work, laughter makes every-one feel good',[1] discusses how leadership, which can occur at all levels of the organisation, is enlightened when it encourages laughter in order to

> *break potentially monotonous routines, to raise the feelgood factor and, importantly, to maintain morale and efficiency in areas when it is all too easy to have one's enthusiasm sapped.*

The *Observer*[2] recently reported on new research findings that are also supporting what we intuitively know yet often suppress at work. An atmosphere of play and laughter correlates positively with creativity and innovation. If people are allowed to use 'larking about' as a way of thinking, they come up with more ideas! These ideas can often save money and significantly contribute to the organisation.

Laughing matters because it is one of the key motivational factors in the workforce and we should encourage it if we want better performance.

WAYS TO THE INNER LAUGHING PLACE

☺ Keep a record of what makes you laugh and share it with others daily. Make sure that you describe the experience and that you do not evaluate it. Don't put yourself or others down.

☺ Learn to give yourself and others permission to laugh for no reason at all.

☺ Know that at times it can help you to mark your experience as 'This is play'. You *can* be full of laughter and thorough in your work and so can others.

☺ Notice how you judge yourself and others when laughter is present in a conversation. Stop it immediately. You are harming your physical and mental health.

☺ Have a way of practising play for the sake of play. So often we even turn our play into work. We feel that we have to run that marathon and win. The purpose becomes the only focus; the process, one for which shortcuts have to be found in order to get to the end. Just like the monkeys, we perform poorly but remain fixated on that banana.

☺ Learn ways to control your mental focus so that you can find the comic in the tragic. This is the essence of the process of reframing, a key life skill to develop for use within work and outside.

☺ Get into the habit of saying, 'This is not funny, but it could be.'

☺ Always ask of a situation 'What else could this mean?' This teaches you to be flexible in your thinking and connect together non-habitual realms of experience, which can more easily lead you to your inner laughing place.

I leave you with a quote from a philosopher who has written extensively about laughter. His name is John Morreal.

For the person who can laugh amusement is valuable not only as a means but as an end, just as any aesthetic experience is. He will not only be amused more often than the serious person, but will enjoy moments of amusement for their own sake. Such a person will often have practical concerns, of course, and will work as well as play. And yet he will not be locked into a practical frame of mind – even while working he will retain his ability to occasionally step back and laugh at the incongruities of life which we encounter everyday. This involves flexibility and openness. In part this flexibility comes from the realisation that what is important is relative to the situation someone is in and to his point of view.

May you find many ways to stop working and start larking about more!

APPENDIX 3

THE LAUGHTER WORKOUT

WARM UP

I have designed this workout to be done with a group of people. You can do it on your own, but you need to be an advanced laugher like Dr Kataria. Few of us have liberated our laughter to such a degree that we can produce it on tap without any social interaction. But it can be done. To help you, on your own or with a group, you may like to have same taped laughter. Comedy shows use them because they work; laughter is contagious. So let's warm up.

☺ Start by pairing up with another person. Facing each other, start gently swaying from back to front. As you do this focus on finding your centre. Now start swaying from side to side very gently. If you find your centre you can keep the gentle movement going without losing balance. After a while, you may find yourself able to do a circle with your body.

☺ Do the monkey. Come to a stop, legs shoulder length apart. Imagine that your are being held from the ceiling by a string. As your back straightens, allow you knees to bend a little. A little more and find yourself standing like a monkey, arms loose by your side, knees bent torso forward. Keep the length of your back as you allow your knees to bend. Stay in that position as long as you can. It won't be for long.

☺ Warm up the face and vocal chords – get your body vibrating to the sound of 'mmmmmmm'. Humming deep for your stomach. Once the hum is going you can add vowels to your mmmm. For example: mmmmaaamamamamamam. Go through all the vowels.

☺ A little singing to put it all together. Any lively song you know. I like *Caballeria Rusticana*, to the words 'many men'.

☺ Finally, not forgetting the brain, sit on the floor facing your partner, hand on your knees. Your task is to reach your nose with your left hand and your left ear with your right hand. Do this at least ten times and as fast as you can. Switch sides and do it faster for another ten times.

☺ If you haven't already started to laugh together, now is time to try a few gentle sounds. Try this all in one breath: Hoo Hoo Hoo/ Haw Haw Haw/ Hee Hee Hee /Hum Hum Hum. Keep with the Hee to the end of your breath. Exaggerate your mouth movements. Open your mouth when you are laughing!

GET GOING

☺ Try this sentence all in one breath:
Do breath tests test breath? Yes,
That's the best of a breath test. Its that the
Best breath stands the breath test best!

☺ Walking 'as if' – let's now all walk around the room. Walking as if we are in different emotional states. Here are some to try: The Angry Walk, The Frustrated Walk, The Happy Walk, The Taking on the World Walk, The Grumpy walk.

☺ Becoming an expert! Choose two non-sense subjects, such as nuns and mushrooms. Your task now is to act as if your are the expert on your subject. Your partner will interview you for national radio. The only rule is that you cannot say the word no.

GONE!

☺ And that reminds me of – Start to talk with your partner. As you are talking and the other gets a thought, any thought, he or she raises a hand and interrupts with 'and that reminds me of …'. As you get a thought, raise the hand and say 'and that reminds me of …'

☺ Find your Laughter Word – we all have triggers to emotions: a song that makes us cry, a smell that makes us feel nostalgic. What is your laughter word? Say it to each other with different voices to help each other laugh.

☺ One minute of laughter – You are now ready to laugh for no reason at all! Help each other keep it going for at least 1 minute. Shut up and laugh! The aim is not to have a conversation.

☺ The number game – Pair up with another pair. Each pair has the task of holding a conversation without words. You are allowed to do everything you would do in a normal conversation but you are to replace words by numbers.

One person starts with '1 2 3.... 4' somebody else answers '5 6...7' and the conversation continues with the numbers going up or down or wherever and each person taking turns. Be as free with your gestures, facial expressions, and voice quality as you wish. And laughter is always allowed, of course.

COMING BACK AND COOLING DOWN

☺ Virtual tickling. Try a minute or two of this. Go towards your partner as if you were about to tickle. Like children, just the thought of tickling can make us laugh.

☺ Make marks on the paper. Find a large piece of paper and some crayons. Make as many marks on the paper as can represent how you are feeling right now. Use as many colours as you need, but not words.

☺ We laugh because we can. Walk slowly together around the room saying as loud and as full of feeling as you dare, 'Let's just laugh because we can.'

RULES OF THE GAME

☺ The workout will only work if you make a conscious choice to put a play frame around it. It does not make sense. It's just a game.

☺ The aim is to laugh as much as possible. If you find yourself stopping the laughter with your hands or with your thoughts or with your breathing, stop it immediately. Let you partner help you keep laughing.

☺ Tell each other 'Shut up and laugh!' as a way of stopping each other talking.

☺ The content of the exercises is non-sense. This is purposeful. It is intended to help you understand that we communicate with so much more than words and that we can make associations between just about anything we choose to.

☺ Focus on liberating your own laughter from conditions. You are not there to make anybody laugh but yourself.

☺ The laughter will come naturally. You don't need to force it. Just look at each other and wait. If all else fails tell each other that 'This is very serious, we must not laugh.' And do your most serious as-if walk.

☺ Take time out if you need to. As we learn to laugh and play we start to re-organise our deepest beliefs. This sometimes means that we need time to integrate what we are learning. You may at times feel uncomfortable and this is okay. It means that you are learning about your emotions. Say 'Welcome' and ask: 'What message do you have for me?' Make a mental note of its words of guidance for you.

☺ Always be respectful of yourself and others. And that means never using the dreaded 'What's the matter with you? Can't you take a joke?' Use your urge to say this as your cue that an apology is due. For whatever reason, you have played with someone else's pain without permission. No, they cannot take your joke, and you owe them an apology.

☺ Have lots and lots of fun together for no apparent reason! It will balance out the many times in the day when you have to act as if you have a reason for everything …

APPENDIX 4

YOUR LIVING THEORY OF LAUGHTER

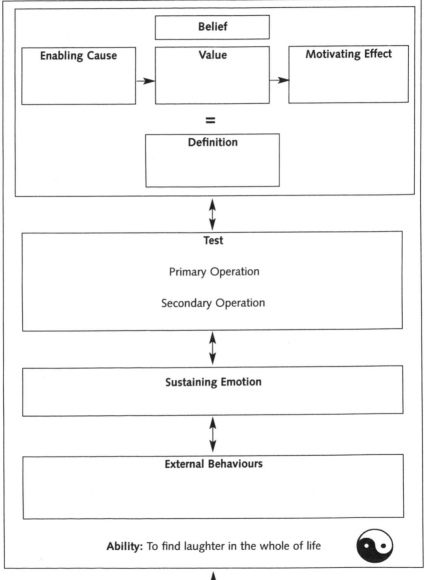

Belief

Enabling Cause → **Value** → **Motivating Effect**

=

Definition

↕

Test

Primary Operation

Secondary Operation

↕

Sustaining Emotion

↕

External Behaviours

Ability: To find laughter in the whole of life

↕

Context
Conversational laughter

NOTES

IN PRAISE OF *LEVITAS*

1 From 'Laughter' by Robert Provine, 1996; published in *American Scientist*. Provine has carried out a lot of primary research on the subject of laughter and writes in a very clear and accessible manner.

2 *Sudden Glory – Laughter as subversive History* by Barry Sanders (Beacon Press, 1995), provides an interesting, though not an easy read, history of laughter.

3 *The Story of The Velveteen Rabbit* by Margery Williams speaks to the heart of what laughter can achieve for us in our lives: belonging and genuine contact with others. We cannot share laughter without sharing ourselves. It is, however, possible to use a one-sided kind of laughter to hurt others, like the other toys in the nursery did with the Rabbit. Visit *www.writepage.com/velvet.htm* for a short version of the story.

CHAPTER 1

1 A new discipline that studies the links between our body, our mind and our emotions. We will explore this in more depth in the next chapter.

2 I have based what follows on the work of Guy Claxton. He has little to say about laughter but much to say about thinking, and as we shall see later on, thinking (defined in a new way) is a necessary condition for laughter. Read his book *Hare brain and tortoise mind: Why intelligence increases when you think less* for a comprehensive review of the experimental data to support the argument I am presenting here.

3 Read 'I had lunch . . .' by Laura Spinney, *New Scientist*, 5 September 1998, if you want an easy review of some of the experiments that these generalisations are based on.

4 Read 'Irresistible Illusions' by Bob Holmes, *New Scientist*, 5 September 1998. He talks about this from the perspective of enhancing our view of thinking and refers to G-mode as the zombie within . . . we really do not like the idea of acting without D-mode knowing.

5 In John Morreal's Essay, p. 107, *Taking Laughter Seriously*, State University of New York, 1983.

6 Umberto Ecco in *The Name of the Rose.*

7 Ibid., p. 107.

8 Arthur Koestler in *The act of creation.* Penguin, 1964, p. 63.

9 Bob Newhart. *Vital Speeches of the Day.* New York; Jul 15, 1997.

10 Quoted in John Morreal, p. 106.

11 Quoted in Max Eastman, *The sense of humor.* Scribners, 1921, p. 188.

CHAPTER 2

1 Mark Frank and Paul Ekman have written an article called 'Not all smiles are created equal: the difference between enjoyment and non-enjoyment smiles' in the journal *Humor* 6-1 (1993), 9-26. They discuss enjoyment smile configuration as having a set of 5 markers: orbicularis oculis involvement in conjunction with zygomatic major (Duchenne's smile), symmetrical action of the zygomatic major, smooth zygomatic major action rather than irregular, duration of zygomatic action that is consistent from one smile to the next, and synchronous action of the zygotic major and the orbicularis oculis such that they reach maximum contraction at the same time. In everyday speech what we are talking about is that the muscles around the face are working together with the muscles around the eyes in genuine responses.

2 Finer distinctions than what follows have been made but this scheme is the most frequently used and comes from the work of H. Pollio, R. Mers and W. Luchesi, 'Humor, laughter and smiling' in J. Godstein (ed) *Psychology of humor,* Academic Press, 1972.

3 A.M. Rankin, P.I. Philip, 1963, 'Epidemic of Laughing in the Bukoba District of Tanganyika', *Central African Journal of Medicine,* 9, 167-170 and also R.R. Provine, 1992, 'Contagious laughter: Laughter is a sufficient stimulus for laughs and smiles', *Bulletin of the Psychonomic Society,* 30:1-4.

4 This quote comes from a great short article by Donald Black called 'Laughter' which has a review of the field.

5 From Pollio et al, ibid.

6 Donald Black, ibid.

7 William Fry, 'The respiratory components of mirthful laughter'.

8 Robert Provine, 'Laughter' *American Scientist,* January-February 1996.

A highly readable account of a very original and informative approach to understanding laughter. A key element I have taken from his work is my own interest in what he calls conversational laughter. An exception to the rule, this paper is able to walk the tightrope of scientific explanation with *levitas* and comes out laughing.

9 Robert Provine, ibid.

10 Charles Darwin. *The expression of emotion in man and animal*, New York, Appleton, 1890.

11 Norman Cousins in 'Anatomy of an illness' talks about laughter as a tool for accessing positive emotions. He assumes that some emotions are negative and, therefore, bad for your health. Whilst I agree on the importance of laughter for our health, I disagree that emotions are negative. I argue, as Candace Pert and Annette Goodheart do, that what has a negative impact on our health is the withholding of our emotions. We may not find grief and anger pleasant, but not pleasant and negative are two different things. We need to learn to not run away from our pain if we are ever to gain emotional health. Labelling emotions as negative and running towards those we like denies half of our emotional reality and will not lead to health.

12 The Impact of Focused Laughter Therapy on Chronic Pain in Young Women with Rheumatoid Arthritis. Unpublished PhD Dissertation, 1994.

13 Ronna Fay Jevne and Alexander Levitan from a book called *No time for nonsense*. Quoted in *The courage to Laugh – Humour, hope and healing in the face of death and dying* by Allen Klein. This book may be an excellent starting point for you to find out just how much laughter can be found in death.

14 Cited in Allen Klein's book. My purpose in sharing these titles with you is to alert you to the existence of a connection between laughter and pain that goes far beyond physical relief aspects. Laughter can not only help us live, it can also help us die, with dignity. If you want the full references, go to the back of his book.

15 See *Humor & Health* November/December, 1994 issue, Volume III, Number 6.

16 PsychoNeuroImmunology Research Society Meetings on April 18, 1996 in Santa Monica, California. In collaboration with Tan.

17 Patty Wotton quoted the research below in her book *Jest for the health of it* published in 1996. The book focuses on the use of laughter for therapeutic purposes in hospital settings.

18 The cathartic model of laughter was first introduced by Spencer and later by Freud. Annette Goodheart uses an adapted version of this model in her therapeutic work. We will look at this model in detail later in this chapter. Read her book *Laughter Therapy*, Real People Press, 1995.

19 'The effect of mirthfulness upon amount of discordant right-left occipital EEG Alpha.' Data showed that there was less discordant brain activity in the 'laughers' group than in the 'non-laughers' group. *Motivation and Emotion*, Vol 6, No 2, 1982.

20 Research cited by Patty Wotton as having been carried out by Derks.

21 *Zen and the Brain*, James H. Austin, MIT Press, 1998.

22 Viennese founder of psychoanalysis: if you want to go to the source for this, it's *Jokes and Their Relation to the Unconscious.*

23 *Zen and the Brain.*

24 Adapted from *Humour and laughter* by M. Apte.

25 R. Hayden on *www.geekcode.com*. Off the scale intensity ratings * means Bliss and ! means Hellish as in '!TV and *T' 'I don't even own a TV and Star Trek is the meaning of life'.

26 *The Molecules of Emotion*, published in 1998. If you read nothing else to follow on from this book, have a look at Candace Pert's book. We have a responsibility to understand what her work means in relation to our physical and emotional health. She is a master at making her subject gripping and relevant.

27 We spoke of Robert Provine's work earlier. He has found that most laughter has little to do with jokes or funny stories. Most laughs in his studies followed mundane statements such as 'It was nice meeting you, too' or, 'Can I join you?', which did not meet 'traditional standards for humour'. Only 10 to 20 per cent of laughter followed a punch line.

CHAPTER 3

1 Adapted from Christina Hall, *The NLP Connection*.

2 Thanks to Joanne Garner for drawing my attention to the link between laughter and TA and for running a workshop with me on this subject.

She brought TA and I brought laughter. We all learned an immense amount.

3 Addisson Wesley, 1971. One of the most accessible introductions to TA available.

4 These words have particular meanings in the theory. To understand the point I'm making you can rely on your intuitive understanding of them. Do read more if you want to go beyond my point that the level at which we connect with people is less in ritual, say, than it is when we play specific psychological games with each other.

5 You may also buy yourself a neat pack of cards titled '52 things to do when you are blue' by Lynn Gordon. The pack contains many useful and fun activities to help you re-connect with your Child (ISBN 0-8118-0661-8).

6 Robert Plutchik has proposed this scheme for the emotions. I like it because it can give us a way of breaking down our emotional experience whilst allowing for many combinations to encapsulate the richness of our emotions. If we factor in duration and intensity, we literally can get hundreds of different emotional states.

7 This is in line with Candace Pert's definition. And, like her, I must also highlight the fact that this is only one definition amongst many. There is significant disagreement amongst experts as to what a comprehensive theory of the emotions would look like.

8 This approach is called Modelling in an area of psychology known as Neuro Linguistic Programming. The techniques that make up this way of working with people are the ones I have used in the interview and in the process that follows. If you are interested in the approach a good introduction is *Modelling in NLP* by Robert Dilts.

9 Adapted from the work of Dilts, 1992 and Gordon and Dawes, 1998.

10 Harvey Mindess in *The use and abuse of humour in psychotherapy* tells this story. I have been familiar with the distinction for quite a while. This was my first experience of the story.

CHAPTER 4

1 A wonderful little book called *There is a hole in my sidewalk* contains this poem. If you can get hold of it, it contains many more poems that

are insightful and light. An excellent example of how self-development need not mean a long face!

2 Downloaded from the World Wide Web on June 7, 1999. I wish I had got to see it!

3 *Completing the Puzzle: The brain-based Approach.* Turning Point Publishing, 1996.

4 This tool has most clearly been outlined in *Reframing* by R. Bandler and J. Grinder.

5 From: Christina Hall, *The NLP Connection*

6 From: Christina Hall, *The NLP Connection*

7 These patterns are based on what are known in Neuro Linguistic Programming as 'Sleight of Mouth Patterns'. If you want to read more detail go to a book called *The Secrets of Magic* by Michael Hall, 1998.

8 Adapted from E. Bandler and W. MacDonald, *An Insider's Guide to Submodalities*, 1988.

9 R. Bandler and J. Grinder, *The Structure of Magic*, 1975.

CHAPTER 5

1 William Fry and Mellanie Allen, 'Humour as a creative experience: The development of a Hollywood humorist.' In Chapman and Foot (eds) *Humor and Laughter. Theory, Research and applications*, Transaction Publishers, 1996.

2 Thomas Moore *On Creativity*, Sounds True Recordings, 1993.

3 Mary Catherine Bateson, *Composing a life*, Plume, 1990.

4 D. Fabum, *You and Creativity*, Glencoe Press, 1969.

5 G. Wallas, *The art of thought*, 1926.

6 Laura Spinner 'I had a hunch ...' *New Scientist*, 5 September, 1998.

7 Bateson. ibid.

8 Mariana Funes and Nancy Johnson, *Honing your Knowledge Skills*, 1998.

9 Guy Claxton referred to G-mode in this way at a workshop of his I attended recently.

10 You may have seen a film by the same name. Patch was played by Robin Williams and was the story of his early years at medical school. His passionate belief that the role of the doctor was to care and that

helping people connect with their laughing place was fundamental to healing and to 'good dying', got him in trouble with the powers that be and almost cost him his degree.

11 Ashleigh Brilliant's Potshots. Write to him at Brilliant Enterprises, 117 W. Valerion Street, Santa Barbara, CA 93101 or phone him on 805 682 0531 and he will send you a starter pack of postcards and a catalogue. The cards are just wonderful reflections on life that never fail to connect me to my laughing place.

12 Angeles Arrien, *The four-fold way*. A book about the fundamental archetypes of life and how to develop them in our being.

13 A friend gave me this quote from a postcard he has. He was unclear about the author.

14 James Carse, *Finite and infinite games: A vision of life as play and possibility*, Penguin, 1986.

15 Guy Claxton uses this term to describe the pattern of perceived data that has been evaluated in a rudimentary fashion.

16 *The Guardian*, May 23, 1998.

17 From *The Celestine Prophecy* by James Redfield, 1993.

18 Unpublished project which I carried out for an organisation of management consultants. In it I made explicit what made this group of people effective at having developmental conversations with their clients. One of the key skills that emerged was the ability to 'stay on the horns of a dilemma' in order to be able to develop creative solutions for a client. The next session is based on this study.

19 From Guy Claxton's book.

20 Edwin Markham. Printed in Steve Andreas's *Is there life before death?* Real People Press, 1995. A delightful book of stories that deserves to be read many times in one's life to be reminded of the 'reason that we are surviving for'.

21 From: *The 5th Discipline*, by Peter Serge. Exercise by W. Isaacs.

22 Normally learned with a teacher in private lessons. There are, however, many books available to introduce you to it. One I particularly recommend is Michael Gelb's *Body Learning*.

23 H. Greenwald in 'Play Therapy for children over 21', *Psychotherapy* Vol 4 no. 1, February 1967.

24 This section is based on games from a wonderful little book called *A book of surrealist games* compiled by A. Brotchie and edited by M. Gooding. Do track it down if you are interested in finding out more about the history of the activities that I suggest in this section.

25 Mel Gooding, ibid.

26 *Magnetic Poetry*© PO Box 14862, Minneapolis, MN 55414, USA. E-mail at *magpo@bitstream.net.* Phone 1-800-720-7269.

27 For example, the one I own is: Poetryslam™ PO Box 1025, Carrboro, NC27510. Phone: 1-919-933-6465. If you want to know more about the actual poetry slam events then try the web: *http://www.com/pep/marc-smith/crowdpleaser/home.html*

28 Mariana Funes and Nancy Johnson, *Honing your Knowledge Skills.*

29 Registered trademark of Waddingtons Games Ltd.

CHAPTER 6

1 From 'The use and abuse of humour in psychotherapy, by Harvey Mindess. In *Humor and Laughter* by Chapman and Foot.

2 If Hamlet had a sense of humor. Harvey Mindess in *It's a funny thing humor* by A.J. Chapman, Pergamon Press, 1977.

3 Fisher K. 'The iconoclast's notebook' *Pschotherapy* 7, 1, 1970.

4 *Orbiting the Giant Hair Ball: A corporate Fool's guide to surviving with grace,* Viking, 1996. A passionate and inspired plea for finding a way to bring our uniqueness to the world and not succumbing to the pull of corporate normalcy. It should be required reading for any manager wanting to make it in the corporate world with soul intact. Viking, 1996.

5 See Appendix 2 'Should we be working or should we be larking?' A short article which I wrote recently applying the ideas of this book to the world of work. Feel free to copy and use it in your battle to orbit the hair ball!

6 'The world of comedy: An introduction to Symposium' by W. Fry in *It's a funny thing humor.*

7 Gordon Allport, *The individual and his religion,* Macmillan, 1950.

8 C. Hyers *Zen and the comic Spirit.* Philadelphia, Westminster, 1973, 127. Quoted in *Zen and the Brain.*

9   Comune-a-key Publishing, 1996. The quotes below come from her book.

10   Annette Goodheart uses this term to refer to the combination of work and play. See her book *Laughter Therapy.*

11   From *Living Downstream* by Sandra Steingraber (www.steingraber.com).

12   'The natural freedom of the mind' by Long-Chen-Pa, 14th Tibetan Buddhist Lama passage quoted in John Morreal's *Taking Laughter Seriously.*

13   From S. Tarpey's MSc dissertation 'In search of fun'. Unpublished.

14   Thank you to Nigel Everett, a participant in one of my workshops, for this little gem.

15   From *Taking laughter seriously* by John Morreal. The paradox of life and laughter is contained in that last sentence. If the emphasis is on 'nothing' then it leads us to detachment. If the emphasis is on 'is' (and I added that emphasis, it was not intended in the original) then it leads us to passionate involvement in the detail of life – the attitude of Detached Attachment that is so key to creating life.

NOTES APPENDIX 2

1   *Financial Times*, 16 June 1999.

2   *Observer*, 18 April 1999.

INDEX

absurd library requests, 205
acronyms and emoticons, 52
adbusters, 207–9
addictions, 148
adult ego-state, 67–72
adulthood, laughter in, ix–x, 1
aerobic fitness, x, 19, 21, 28
affect (emotions), 11
Alexander, Mathias, 64
Alexander technique, 64, 164
Allen, Woody, 195
Allport, Gordon, 235n
ambiguity, 158
American Association for
    Therapeutic Humour, 206
anchoring process, 84
anger, 78–9, 81
ankylosing spondylitis, 26
anti-inflammatory effect of laughter,
    xi, 19, 26
Apte, M., 231n
Arrien, Angeles, 148, 234n
arthritic conditions, 26
Austin, James H., 231n
automatic writing, 130, 169

Bain, Alexander, 39
Bateson, Mary Catherine, 138,
    144–5, 156
behaviour, 11
    determinants of, 4–9
beliefs, 89
    and behaviour, 11
    changing your deterministic
        belief, 108–111
    conscious, 10
    and g-mode thinking, 10–11
    and laughter, 1–2, 97–100

personal choice of, 96
    that limit laughter, 119–21
belly laugh, 22, 25
Benigni, Roberto, 58, 64
Bergson, Henri, 39
Berk, Lee, 31, 35
beta-endorphins, ix
bissocative thinking, 15, 154, 170,
    176, 188
Black, Donald, 20, 229n
blood pressure, ix, 18, 30
Body Learning, 234n
body-mind connection, xi, 55–7, 76,
    107, 228n
boredom, 117–18
Born to Win, 69
Bowie, David, 171
brain-damaged patients, 9–10, 20,
    42
brain design, 106
brainwashing, 14
Breton, Andre, 169
Brillant, Ashleigh, 234
Buscaglia, Leo, 60, 201

Carse, James, 167, 234n
category game, 115–16, 154
cathartic activities, 35–6, 42, 76–7,
    77, 79–80, 231n
Chaplin, Charlie, 58, 64
child, developing a connection with
    your, 72–3
child ego-state, 67–72
childhood, laughter in, ix–x, 1
Cicco, Robert, 206
Claxton, Guy, 7, 150, 152, 228n
clown, playing the, vi, 140, 150,
    188–94

cognition, current research in, 152
communication strategies, xii, 80–85
Compassionate Laughter, 193
conversational laughter, vi, 57, 218
conversational literacy, 126, 136
corporate culture, 99–100,
    190–191, 197
cortisol levels, x, 18
Cosby, Bill, 36
Courage to Laugh, The, 230n
court jester, role of, vi, 140, 150,
    188–94
Cousins, Norman, 26, 34, 56, 230n
creative paradox, 187, 190–191
creative tension, 156–9, 165, 192
creativity, 233n
    10 key traits of in people, 182–3
    in context of work, 176–9,
        180–182
    and g-mode/d-mode thinking,
        142–3
    and language, 176–9
    and laughter, xiii, 137
    stages in, 142–5
    tips for in everyday life, 183–4
    what it is, 137–41
crying, 37, 44, 85, 186
Csikszentmihalyi, Mihaly, 182
cultural values *see also* corporate
    culture
    and laughter, 7–8, 13–14
curiosity, xiii, 140–141

daily life
    complexity of, 156
    laughter in, 101–2
    narrative for, 148, 151–3
Darwin, Charles, 230n
death/dying and laughter, vi–vii,
    29–30, 79, 103, 172
decision making, 160–161

D(eliberate)-mode thinking *see also*
    G(ap) mode thinking, 6–9, 10,
    11, 92
    and g-mode interaction, 44–6,
        57, 98–9, 156, 186, 228n
    and analysing problems,
        150–151
    and laughter barriers, 96–8
depression, 15, 60
depth ambiguity, 158
dilemmas, how to deal with,
    157–60, 161, 163, 201, 234n
dingbats, 180–181, 211–12

e-mail and emotional expression,
    49–50, 198–200
educators, 5
effective learning, 8, 11–12
efficiency, letting go of, 153–4
Ekman, Paul, 229n
Elliot, T. S., 74
Emerson, Ralph Waldo, 146
emoticons, 46, 49–50, 51–2
emotional cycle, 75–80
emotional health, and immune
    system, 34–5
emotional intelligence, 85, 145
emotional literacy, xi, 37–8, 142
    development of, 54–7
emotional release, 38, 41–4, 55,
    77–8, 80
emotional understanding, 44–6
emotions, xii, 107
    and creativity, 142, 144–5
    and g-mode/d-mode thinking,
        142
    and language, 47–9
    primary, 76
    theory of, 232n
endorphins, 18, 27–8, 34
enjoyment smile configuration, 19

Erasmus, 15
exploratory drive, 7, 76, 140–141, 144–5, 155, 158
exquisite corpse and related games, 170, 173

Fay, William, 22, 214
fear, 81
finite/infinite games, 166–8, 234n
Fisher, K., 235n
focused laughter therapy, 27, 230n
folly, 15
fool, role of, 140, 150, 188–94
frame of play, 11, 41, 58
and pain, 84–5
frame shifting activity, 62–3
framing/reframing, 112–14, 125–6, 155, 232n
context reframe, 115
meaning reframe, 114
Frank, Mark, 229n
Frankl, Victor, 15, 36, 192
Freud, Sigmund, 41, 42, 174
Fritz, Robert, 157
Fry, William, xi, 63, 192, 229n

games, xiv, 97, 166–8, 168–75, 235n
G(ap)-mode thinking see also D(eliberate) mode thinking, 6–9, 10, 11, 92
and ability to learn and think, 12
awareness of, 16
development of, 72
and shifting psychological states, 44–6
Garner, Joanne, 69, 231n
Gazzaniga, Michael, 5, 14, 146
geekcode, 52–4
Gibran, Kahlil, 60
Glaser, Janice and Roland, 33
Global Ideas Bank, 207

Goodheart, Annette, 26, 42, 43, 81–2, 85, 230n, 231n, 236n
Gooding, M., 235n
Gordon, Lynn, 232n
gravitas, vi–vii, 100, 104
Greeks, the, vi
grief, 79, 81

habitual action/thought, 154, 155, 157, 164
Hall, Christina, 231n
Hamlet, 187
healing laughter, 66–72, 156
and beliefs, 96–8
communication strategies for, 80–85
Herchenhorn, Suzanne, 27
Hitler, Adolf, 13
Hobbes, Thomas, 38
Holmes, Bob, 228n
Holmes and Rahe Social Readjustment Scale, 94
human laughter response, ix, 16
humour, xi–xii
and creativity, 137, 146
five different types of, 65–7
Humour & Health (journal), 230n
Humour and Laughter, 235n
Humour (journal), 229n
hurtful laughter, xi–xii, 214

illness and laughter see also terminal illness, 29–30, 230n
imagination, xiii, 12
immune system, x, 18, 28–9, 30–31, 31, 34, 35
immunoglobulin, , 18, 33
in-group feeling, 218
In Praise of Folly, 15–16
incongruity theory, 38, 39–40, 44, 55

Indian Laughing Club, xiv, 205–6
individuality, 149
indoctrination, 14
infinite/finite games, 166–8, 234n
inner laughing place, 16, 30, 59, 61,
    102, 145, 214
    ways to, 96, 221
Ionesco, Eugene, 194
Irish wakes, 102–5
Irwin, Michael, 33
Is there life before death?, 234

James, Murial, 69
Jensen, Eric, 106
Jest for the Health of it, 231n
jester, role of, vi, 140, 150, 188–94
jokes, vi, 20, 41, 63, 139
Jongeward, Dorothy, 69
joy, 91, 92, 93

Kant, Immanuel, 39–40
Kataria, Dr. Madan, xiv, 205–6, 223
Klein, Allen, 230
knowledge, our ideas of, 146–7
knowledge transfer skills, 146
Kobassa, Suzanne, 36
Koestler, Arthur, 7, 14, 40, 138–40,
    154, 176

language, 2
    and creativity, 176–9
    of laughter, 119–21
    of thought, 12, 176–7
larking, 213
Laughing Clubs of India, xiv, 205–6
laughter *see also* healing laughter,
    learning, living theory of
    laughter, vi, xiii
    anthropological view of, 23–4
    barriers to, xii–xiii, 96–100,
        108–111, 217–22

in daily life, 101–2
    dark side of, 65
    difference in intensity of, 19
    effects on the body, 18, 19–22,
        25–6
    and ego-states, 67–75
    five different types of, 65–7
    list of what makes, 3
    and mixed emotions, 186
    patterns, 121–5
    purposes of, 185–6
    questions, 81–4
    reasons for, 6, 215–16
        emotional release, 41–4
        feelings of superiority, 38–9
        g-mode and pleasant shifts,
            44–6
        perception of incongruity,
            39–41
        research findings, 9–11, 21–2,
            31–4, 32–4, 220
    rules of, 13–14
    self-referential, 101–2
    as a sign, 2–3, 8–9
    situations when it occurs, 20
    sound of, 22, 23–4
    therapeutic effects of, 26–30
    and work ethics, 99–100, 123–15,
        197, 218–19
    workout, 207, 223–6
    workshops, xiv, 15, 61, 107,
        213–14
Laughter Therapy, 231n
learning, 8, 10–12
    and laughter, 106–8
    theory of, 5
Lefcourt, Herb, 34, 217
Levine, Stephen, 61
levitas, vi–vii, 64, 69, 99–100, 147,
    207
Levy, Julian, 168

life, making sense of, 151–3, 154–7
limbic system, 27–8
Living Downstream, 194–5
living theories, contradictory, 1, 167
living theory of laughter, 85
  developing personal guidelines
    for, 86–9
  example of, 91–5
  structure for, 90, 94, 227
Locke, Steven, 33
locus of control, ix, 13, 16
luxury reflex, 14, 139

MacKenzie, Gordon, 190–191, 200
magical thinking cycle, xii, 75–7, 79
mental imagery, ways of
  articulating, 126–30
meta-model patterns, 130–136
  game, 134
  questions, 131, 135
metaphors, 176–7
mind-body connection, xi, 55–7, 76,
  107, 228n
Mindess, Harvey, 187, 189, 232n,
  235n
mistakes, 147
modality language *see also*
  submodality language, 126–7
Molecules of Emotion, The, 231n
mood-altering drugs, 59
Moody, Ray, 65
Moore, Thomas, 138, 149–50, 153
Morreal, John, 209–10, 221–2,
  236n
  theory of laughter, 44–5
motivational levels, 219
muscular tension, x, 18, 21, 30
Myss, Caroline, 110

narrative for daily life, 148, 151–3,
  177

Nelson, Portia, 101
neuro linguistic programming, 232n,
  233n
Newhart, Bob, 15, 229n
newspaper headlines, comic, 201–2
Niebuhr, R., 198
non-habitual associations, xiv, 45–6,
  168
non-verbal messages, 49
North Whitehead, Alfred, 29

on-line communication, 49–55
Orbiting the Giant Hair Ball, 235

pain relief, x, xi–xii, 18
  effects of laughter and, 26–30
  and emotions involved, 43–4
  playing with respectfully, 58–63,
    84–5, 103–4
paradox of life and laughter, 21,
  236n
paradoxical intention, 192–4
paradoxical world views, 1, 167
parent ego-state, 67–72
Parker, Dorothy, 185
Patch Adams, 147, 206, 233n
pathological laughter, 42
peer pressure, 149–50, 218
Pert, Candace, 28, 34, 55, 60, 75,
  76, 85, 230n, 231n
Philip, P. I., 229n
physiological bases for laughter, x
Picabia, Francis, 198
Picasso, Pablo, 149
Plato, 13
play, true, xiii, 64, 66, 104–1
play frame, xi–xii, 63, 200
  and creativity, 166–8
  and work, 214–5
play in adult life, 8, 155
pleasure, society's view of, 197

Plutchik, Robert, 232n
poetry games/events, 171–2,
    232–3n, 235n
Pollio, R., 20, 229n
Post-Its'®, laughter, 197–8
Potshots©, 147
problems see also decision making,
    180–181
    attachment/detachment from,
        159–60
    multiple perspectives on, 161–6
    types of, 150–151
Protestant work ethic, 63, 197
Provine, Robert, 23–4, 218, 228,
    229–30n, 231n
psychogeography, awareness of, 86,
    89
psychology and child/adult laughter,
    ix, 1–2
Psychology of Humour, 229n
psychoneuroimmunology, 4, 34, 56,
    60, 154, 230n
psychotherapy, 189–90

Quixote, Don, 39

Rankin, A. M., 229n
reality cycle, xii, 75–7, 79
redefinition game, 117–119
Redfield, James, 234n
relaxation see also stress, x, 18
relief theories, 38, 41–4, 55, 76–7,
    80
Robinson, Robbie, 61

Saltzman, David, 58
Sanders, Barry, 228n
Sandra Steingraber, 194–5
Sargent, William, 14
Satir, Virginia, 86
Saussure, Dr Ferdinand, 2

Schooler, Jonathan, 143
Scott, Sir Neville, 8
selection theory, 5
self-worth
    choice of 'way we are,' 111–14
    development of, 108–111, 151–3
Selye, Hans, 35, 36
semantics, 176
semiotics, 2–4
Serge, Peter, 234n
Sharma, Sumit, 205
Shepard, Roger, 166
shifting frames of reference, 63
signs
    assigning meaning to, 4–6
    study of, 2–4
Silbermann, Jean Claude, 172
societal messages, response to, 14
Sopault, Philippe, 169
Spencer, Herbert, 40, 42
Spinney, Laura, 228n
spiritual teachers, 193–4
spontaneity, 21
Steingraber, Sandra, 236n
stereograms, 165
stereotypes, 38–9, 41, 63–4
Stravinsky, Igor, 138
stress, 41, 75–6, 85, 123, 215–16
    effects of, 216–17, 219
    effects of laughter on, 30–31, 35
    interpretation of, 36–7
    susceptibility to, 94
sub-modality language, 128–130,
    233n
suffering see pain relief
super-ego, the, 41–2
superiority theories, 38–9, 44, 55,
    63
surrealist games, xiv, 168–75, 235n
Svebak, Sven, 37

Tarpey, Steve, 197, 236
tears, viii, 18, 21
Tehee Practice, 83
tension, creative, 156–9, 165, 192
terminal illness and laughter, 103
therapists, 189–90
thought
    flexibility of, 155
    modes of, 5–6
    structure of, 126–30
Tibetan Lama, 195, 236n
tragi-comic model, 186–7
transactional analysis, 67–72,
    231–2n
Tree of Life, 59
true play, xiii, 64, 66, 140–141

unconscious understanding, 5, 8
unhealed feeling, 75–7, 79

virtual communication, 49–55

wakes, 102–5
Wallas, G., 143
Wilde, Oscar, 40, 41, 185
Williams, Margery, 228n
wisdom and laughter, 145, 194–7
women and men who make them
    laugh, 100–102
Wooton, Patty, 193, 231n
work and laughter, 99–100, 197,
    213–15, 218–19
    and creativity, 176–9, 180–182
workplace, useful phrases in, 203–4
World Laughter Day, 206

Zen, vi–vii, 193, 231n, 235n

CONTACT INFORMATION

I have become a reluctant laughter educator. I never wanted to spend my days doing activities that 'were not serious' or that 'did not make me feel concerned with matters of consequence'. I have, over time, learnt to redefine what counts as matters of consequence and this book reflects my learning.

As I run my workshops and talk to anyone interested about why Laughing Matters, I am always asked for 'hard and serious' evidence that what I suggest is worth considering.

If you use this book to help yourself live more creatively with laughter, do write to me and let me know your story, what bits particularly helped you and how you have used them.

If you tried some activity and it did not work for you, I'd appreciate hearing what else I could add in terms of explanation to make it easier for others to use in the future.

It would just be good to hear about you and why laughing matters in your life!

I can be contacted via my publishers:

Gill & Macmillan
Hume Avenue
Park West
Dublin 12
Ireland

Or via email: laughingms@aol.com